"*Stories of Sifted* is a tremendou[s ...] and others on your team. It re[minds ...always], and continues to, use the troubles and hardships of His people to increase our surrender to Him. Increased surrender is the seed that produces 100X fruitful multiplication through us. Jesus promised the troubles AND He promised that our resulting faithfulness would produce 100X impact and fruitfulness. We are sifted for multiplication. Read this book and grow through times of sifting to become a healthier reproducing leader for many years to come!"

—**Dave Ferguson**, New Thing

"Planting a church is possibly the loneliest, hardest thing on the planet. No pastor should do it alone. *Stories of Sifted* provides inspiration and encouragement for the journey."

—**Rick Warren**, Saddleback Church

"I'm so encouraged that these real-world stories of increased surrender during times of trouble are now available in book form. They will challenge and inspire you in the real work of church planting!"

—**Ed Stetzer**, Executive Director, Billy Graham Center at Wheaton College

"My first church plant closed its doors as quickly as we began. As painful and as difficult as that experience was for my wife and me, we were *sifted* in a way that prepared us for even greater fruit in the future. *Stories of Sifted* is filled with inspiring and encouraging stories of how God uses our faithfulness and increased surrender through troubles for His glory. This resource will give you a new paradigm for our worldly troubles."

—**Mark Batterson**, National Community Church

"It's no fun being sifted. But it's absolutely essential. From the first pages of the Bible on, the people God has used for His glory have all been sifted. It's His way of separating the wheat from the chaff. Consider these stories, dwell on them and learn from them. They can save much heartache and provide much power."

—**Larry Osborne**, North Coast Church

"The Bible tells us to recognize those who refresh our spirits, those 'devoted to the service of the Lord's people' (I Corinthians 16:15-18). *Stories of Sifted* brings encouragement and perspective to those engaged in the hard work of expanding God's Kingdom. Thank you, Todd and Eric, for lifting our spirits!"

—**Tom Nebel**, Speaker, Author, Church Planting Coach

"As a younger leader, you tend to skip the sifted verses, thinking 'that wouldn't happen to me.' When you are a seasoned leader (code word for older), you tend to linger on the sifted verses, thinking, 'if they can stay strong in their faith, my valley isn't that deep. ' I love the creativity of putting these familiar Bible passages into the first person."

—**George Klippenes**, Veteran Church Planter and Coach

"Church planting is as much about what God is doing in the life and heart of the planter as it is about reaching lost people because God uses the crucible of planting to form his character in those He calls to plant. *Stories of Sifted* presents the rest of the church planting story we all need to know. A must-read for any aspiring church planter!"

—**Steve Pike,** Founder of Urban Islands Project

STORIES *of* SIFTED

Increased Surrender During Times of Trouble

Eric Reiss and Todd Wilson *with Jan Greggo*
Foreword by Wayne Cordeiro | Epilogue by Bob Buford

an ⹂EXPONENTIAL⹃
Series Resource

ΞXPONENTIAL

Stories of Sifted: Increased Surrender During Times of Trouble
Copyright © 2019 by Eric Reiss, and Todd Wilson with Jan Greggo

Distributed via Exponential Resources

Exponential is a growing movement of leaders committed to the multiplication of healthy new churches. Exponential Resources spotlights and spreads actionable principles, ideas and solutions for the accelerated multiplication of healthy, reproducing faith communities. For more information, visit exponential.org

All rights reserved. No part of this book may be reproduced in any manner whatsoever without prior written permission from the publisher, except where noted in the text and in the case of brief quotations embodied in critical articles and reviews.

This book is manufactured in the United States.

Unless otherwise indicated, Scripture quotations marked (NIV) are taken from the Holy Bible, New International Version®, NIV®. Copyright © 1973, 1978, 1984, 2011 by Biblica, Inc.™ Used by permission of Zondervan. All rights reserved worldwide. http://www.zondervan.com

Scripture quotations taken from the New American Standard Bible®, Copyright © 1960, 1962, 1963, 1968, 1971, 1972, 1973, 1975, 1977, 1995 by The Lockman Foundation. Used by permission." (www.Lockman.org)

All emphases in Scripture quotations have been added by the authors.

ISBN-13: 978-1-62424-029-4 (Print)

Credits
Foreword: Wayne Cordeiro
Epilogue: Bob Buford
Cover Design: Karen Pheasant
Interior Design: Harrington Interactive Media
Editor: Lindy Lowry

ACKNOWLEDGMENTS

E (Eric Reiss) would like to thank Todd for asking me to be a part of this project. It's one of the most interesting and rewarding spiritual exercises I've taken in years. I'd also like to thank my beautiful girls, Karen and Evangeline, for their support in more ways than I could name. And a huge thank you to God, for letting me live a life that is blessed beyond anything I could have dreamed.

Todd is grateful to his wife, Anna, and boys, Ben and Chris, who are regularly the beneficiaries of the worldly troubles that come through the sifting of full-time vocational ministry.

Todd and Eric would also like the thank the team of dedicated servants at Exponential who sacrificially give themselves to make resources like this available.

Finally, many people have contributed to the research necessary to develop the Bible leader stories of sifted. Thank you to Mike Fewster, Creed Branson, Dave Baldwin, Anna Mari Green, Jan Greggo and Mark Boughner.

EXPONENTIAL
RESOURCING CHURCH PLANTERS

- 90+ eBooks
- Largest annual church planting conference in the world (Exponential Global Event in Orlando)
- Regional Conferences - Boise, DC, Southern CA, Bay Area CA, Chicago, Houston and New York City
- Exponential Español (spoken in Spanish)
- FREE Online Multiplication & Mobilization Assessments
- FREE Online Multiplication & Mobilization Courses
- Conference content available via Digital Access Pass (Training Videos)
- Weekly Newsletter
- 1000+ Hours of Free Audio Training
- 100s of Hours of Free Video Training
- Free Podcast Interviews

exponential.org

Twitter.com/churchplanting
Facebook.com/churchplanting
Instagram.com/church_planting

CONTENTS

Foreword by Wayne Cordeiro 9

Introduction 13

SECTION 1: STORIES OF SIFTED
Seeing Sifting Through the Eyes of Bible Leaders 17

DISCOURAGEMENT

1 | Joshua Sifted..21
2 | Lot Sifted 25
3 | Ruth Sifted...29
4 | Boaz Sifted 33
5 | Peter Sifted..39
6 | Elijah Sifted...55
7 | Hosea Sifted 61
8 | Job Sifted...65
9 | Paul Sifted 69

PERSONAL CHARACTER

10 | Adam Sifted 75
11 | Abraham Sifted 79
12 | Isaac Sifted 83
13 | Jacob Sifted 87
14 | Joseph Sifted..91

15	Moses Sifted	95
16	Samson Sifted	99
17	Saul Sifted	105
18	David Sifted	109
19	Jonah Sifted	113

DOUBT AND FEAR

20	Noah Sifted	119
21	Gideon Sifted	127
22	Daniel Sifted	131
23	Esther Sifted	135
24	Nehemiah Sifted	139
25	John the Baptist Sifted	143
26	Jesus Sifted	147

SECTION 2: FOUNDATIONS IN SIFTING

Defining the Nature and Scope of Sifting 155

27	Why Sifted?	157
28	What Is Sifting	161
29	Jesus on Sifting	165
30	Paul on Sifting	171
31	Causes & Symptoms	177
32	Spiritual Warfare	183
33	Multiplication	189
34	Your Story of Sifted	195

Epilogue from Bob Buford 201

About the Authors 205

FOREWORD

*God must do something powerful in you
before He can do something powerful through you.*

As both children of God and leaders in ministry, we can find comfort, strength and peace in knowing that God has a purpose for our difficult seasons of sifting—refinement. A "sifted" person can look back on his trials with perspective. He emerges from the process wise, tested, capable and more mature, equipped to compassionately encourage others in their troubles.

Ultimately, our prayer is *not* that we would be spared from sifting, but rather that we would navigate the process well. And that when this season passes, our faith would thrive and that we would strengthen our brothers as a result (Luke 22:31).

Even at this late date in my life, God is taking me through an additional sifting process. It's a journey that continues today into eternity.

I had not been feeling well for about a year and after many medical appointments and a battery of tests, we found out why. I was diagnosed with cancer in the intermediate stage. I needed to act quickly, but the "C" word had me polarized. There was nothing I could do to make it go away. I prayed, fasted, begged and asked hundreds to pray for me. However, I knew I had to face the reality of surgery.

While praying (or rather begging), I heard these words: "God is a good God and He cares."

Being sifted is not the easiest thing to do, but I was determined to keep my eyes on Jesus through the whole experience. I had to trust in His goodness because there was simply no other way. I often say, *"Sometimes you don't realize that Jesus is all you need until Jesus is all you got!"* This was one of those times.

I had the surgery a month after the diagnosis and am now in remission. I still need to take tests every three months, but I am glad to be living and still learning that God is a good God and He cares!

Let's make this personal. If you are serious about following Christ, you *will* be sifted. Paul alludes to this truth as he counsels his protégé, Timothy. "Indeed, all who desire to live godly in Christ Jesus will be persecuted" (2 Timothy 3:12 NASB).

Will *you* be able to navigate the sifting process well and emerge from the other side strengthened? That›s the big question. Will you have the skills, patience and depth of spiritual life to survive the sifting?

Pastoring is not always easy. It gets lonely and discouraging. Even without Satan's mischievous schemes, our worldly struggles would be hard enough. We can't make it without God's help. Fortunately, He has filled the Bible with stories of leaders we can learn from—leaders who were sifted, just as we, and emerged more surrendered and stronger to do God's work. God is not calling us to do or endure anything that he has not exposed His servants to throughout time.

I'm thrilled to have this Book, *Stories of Sifted*, as a supplemental resource to what I believe is one of my most important books, *Sifted:*

Pursuing Growth through Trials, Challenge, and Disappointments (Exponential Series with Zondervan Publishing).

Stories of Sifted will inspire and encourage you, as it has me. It will remind you that a «great cloud of witnesses» has come before you—men and women who have experienced the same struggles and problems you may be going through now. Recognize that as you fight the good fight and emerge stronger, you become part of the great cloud of witnesses, sifted to encourage others today and in the future. You are chosen. You are loved. God will sustain and grow you through your increased surrender to Him.

Dr. Wayne Cordeiro

INTRODUCTION

Why did we write this book?

At some point in your life, you will feel discouraged, lonely, disconnected, possibly like a failure. Quitting or giving up will seem like viable options. In seasons like these, remember this truth: You're not alone. Great leaders on the world stage and those working silently behind the scenes have struggled in the same exact ways. Struggles and trials are a part of everyone's lives. Our goal in writing *Stories of Sifted* is to look at these difficult seasons in a new way.

We also were thinking of church multipliers and the cycle they go through of vision, strategy, implementation and somewhere along the way–sifting. There's no way around it. Sifting is hard and incredibly discouraging. It is a crucible of the soul. As we are sifted, it's very common to think about walking away to try or do something else easier than starting a church.

The approach we've taken:

We wrote *Stories of Sifted* in two primary sections. Section 1 is in a narrative format, intended to be a guide for encountering familiar stories in a fresh way. You'll find 30 stories of biblical leaders, told from their point of view, and imagining their experience in personal, honest and relevant ways. We purposed to put on their shoes, walk in their footsteps and see through their eyes. The goal was to learn from their lives in ways that could enrich our own, to vicariously experience their struggles and loss, their successes and hopes. It went better than we ever imagined and deeper than we ever expected.

The danger with this kind of exercise lies in the potential to distract from the power Scripture has in our lives directly. Please know we don't intend for these stories to replace anything written in Scripture or to hold up these perspectives and insights as historically true. Instead, consider these character profiles a thoughtful meditation on the familiar stories in three topical areas: the pain of Discouragement; the molding of Personal Character; and the struggle of Fear and Doubt.

Section 2 moves from the heart to the head and offers a look at foundational principles that will help us form a different paradigm about sifting. What is the basic idea? What are its boundaries? Why is sifting important? How are we defining the idea of sifted, and how does it play out in the larger context of a spiritual journey and ministry? These few chapters are meant to orient us with definition, direction and a frame of reference.

Here's what we hope to see:

God is writing a story of your life. Inevitably, part of that story is sifting. The goal of this book is to help you understand that sifting isn't something to be avoided, but rather a process to participate in and actively embrace. Changing our thinking about sifting and what it means will help us move from discouragement to joy.

Don't hold this process at arm's length. Let the stories you read impact you emotionally and resonate with your own. Learn from these leaders' mistakes. Rejoice in their victories. Reflect on their brokenness. Find resonance in their greatness of heart and witness their faith in a God who loves them in every circumstance.

Know that He loves you, too. Know in your bones that He will never forsake you. Know that His plan is for you to be everything He has created you to be.

Even as you are sifted.

SECTION ONE

STORIES OF SIFTED

Seeing Sifting Through the Eyes of Bible Leaders

DISCOURAGEMENT

CHAPTER 1

Joshua Sifted

I'm called by God. I know that more than I know anything.

I've been mentored by some of the best leaders of my generation.

I've had early success; God has blessed my efforts and the people I've gotten to lead.

I'm restless. I'm ready. I want to act. The door allowing me to step out hasn't opened.

How long do I have to wait?

That question has haunted my life. I believe that God is powerful. I believe that God can do whatever He wants. I believe that His purposes are good and that He can accomplish anything.

I don't always believe in this group of people around me. They are fickle, faithless and afraid. They are also amazing, bold and full of life and love. I don't know how they can be both at the same time, but somehow, they are.

From the golden calf to the constant complaining, this generation would actually prefer to wander in the desert, eating scraps from God's table instead of feasting at the banquet He has prepared. We are capable of so much more, if I could just get them to see it.

He is capable of so much more, if I could just get them to believe.

Caleb shares my frustration and has little patience for this foolishness. He's often asked why God doesn't leave us and start over. I don't have a good answer for that one.

When we returned from our initial reconnaissance, the path forward was clear. This was the land God had promised to Abraham and to us. Either God's Word is good, or it isn't. Why are we still talking about this?

I know God loves Israel, and we are His own. His power has parted the seas, and His provision has kept us alive. I just wonder if anything will ever really change. What will they need to see or experience before they know that God is who He claims to be? If only they could know Him like Moses and I do, if they could experience His presence around the ark, if only they could hear His voice, things would be so different.

I am grateful for His provision. We are fed by bread from heaven and would die without it, but I secretly long for the day when He leads us to feed ourselves. We're training to that end, Caleb and I. Focusing on the children and the younger men, we're teaching them to run and to fight. We're teaching them moving formations and how to operate together as a team. We're also teaching them to pray and believe. They're tough and motivated, these children of the desert. Thin and browned by the unending sun, they have a quiet strength borne of knowing what it is to be thirsty. Honestly, I'm glad they're on my side. Not everyone sees them like I do. Maybe we can go ahead and bring the others along later. I honestly don't know what God is waiting on. With His power, we're as ready as we ever will be.

How long do I have to wait?

Like our nation, I know that I personally am capable of more than I'm currently doing. I would never dishonor my teacher and mentor, but I feel like God has called me to more, and I'm weary of what seems a pointless journey. Men are blessed through my insight and organization. They are capable of doing and being even more than they see in themselves. I see their potential through God's eyes, and I can help push them to be even more than they ever imagined.

When will I get my chance to move? When will I get to be in a role that makes the most of God's plan for my life? When will the waters part for me and deliver me to His best?

Moses is fond of saying that if you pray for patience, God will make you wait for it. I suppose that's true enough. I know my heart is in line with His heart. I want what He wants more than my next breath.

I'm just tired of waiting. God's timing is mysterious and hard for me to understand.

> *"This book of the law shall not depart from your mouth, but you shall meditate on it day and night, so that you may be careful to do according to all that is written in it; for then you will be prosperous, and then you will have success. Have I not commanded you? Be strong and courageous! Do not tremble or be dismayed, for the Lord Your God is with you wherever you go"* (Joshua 1:8-9).

CHAPTER 2

Lot Sifted

Some stories don't have a beautiful ending.

I can still feel the angels' hands pulling us urgently out of the city. They told us to never look back. They told us!

In a moment, the shape of my life twisted. I no longer had a loving wife to grow old with me. I wouldn't get to lay her to rest in a cave, adorned by flowers and incense and song. She was pulled from my side on the day of His judgment, without honor and without appeal. The salt from my tears is a stinging reminder of her turning away from God to look back. She turned away from us as well, from my daughters and me. That horrible moment is burned in my memory forever.

Even then, the divine hands of the supernatural gripped me tightly, strengthening me beyond my ability to bear it. It was firm but loving in an understanding kindness that swept us along, step upon step to safety. But she was still lost to me.

We didn't have the child of promise. My daughters are far from God and drifting. I don't know if that will ever change. They were widowed that day, too. My sorrow is like the stars in the sky and the sand beside the sea, thoughts of sadness without number.

Stories of Sifted

My story is not one of success or greatness or legacy. My children are not the stuff God will use to build the nations. My story is the sad tale of an average man who is steadfast and wholly committed to God. In spite of faith, my days here will end in heartbreak and sorrow. I would give almost anything to have Abraham's story, to have the tragedy averted in the last moment as God brings provision and blessing. To have the circumstances reversed and the one who loses everything finds God's blessing and provision and power.

For me, that isn't how it was written.

My men have left me for better work. My flocks have dwindled. My wife is gone. My daughters executed an evil scheme to get what they wanted, though I don't remember it.

My palace is a forgotten cave, secluded and alone and here is where I die. I have been faithful to God, but my story is one of the hardest lessons of all.

I grieve my loss and my family, but you must know that I don't grieve as one who has no hope. I trust Him. And I will continue to trust Him. Do you understand why?

Abraham told me of the conversation he had with God over Sodom and Gomorrah, after it was all over.

What if there are 50 righteous people?

What if there are 10 righteous people?

And if He didn't say it, I still think God's heart was clear enough.

What if there is one righteous person?

That person was me.

God sent angels to rescue my family and me. In the Day of Judgment and destruction, He sent us help from heaven itself. It wasn't just for Abraham; God came because of His love for me.

He loves me.

He loves me as much as He loves Abraham. When I lie with my fathers and these eyes close for good, I will stand on the shores of eternity with my uncle at my side . . . and I will glorify God and enjoy Him forever. That doesn't make it easy, but it does give me hope.

Some stories don't have a beautiful ending.

Don't lose heart. Some stories are finally beautiful, but their beauty lies beyond the chapter of what we know, told in His words, beyond what we can see.

> *"So, when God destroyed the cities of the plain, he remembered Abraham, and he brought Lot out of the catastrophe . . ."*
> (Genesis 19:29a).

CHAPTER 3

Ruth Sifted

With the loss of my husband, it strikes me how much my life has been altered. That ending wasn't part of my storybook plan. It was so unexpected, and all of the things I imagined were cut off in an instant. All of life's plans only made sense in the context of this other person to share them with. When a spouse is removed from the picture, everything else seems empty.

The dream I had of family and children and children's children died with my husband. I didn't know what life had for me now. I had no home of my own. The ties to my old life in my father's house had been cut, and I felt like I was adrift in a sea of emotion and endless grief.

And even worse, I had come to know and love the God of Israel. The stories of the great men of faith and their adventures from Abraham to Isaac to Jacob to Joseph thrilled me and resonated in my heart of hearts. I felt like I knew them, and I couldn't get away from the realization that the gods of my fathers were false and poor imitations of the real God in heaven. I couldn't go back to my father's house. There was no place for me there now.

Years passed. When Naomi told me she was going back to Bethlehem, I had no choice but to go with her. That moment crystallized what I already knew. Naomi was my home now.

The God of Abraham, Isaac and Jacob was the God of Ruth as well.

So off we went… she back to a place she left so many years ago, and I, a stranger in a strange land, yearning for a love I would never know.

We arrived in Bethlehem and settled in, eventually connecting with the poor, seeking benevolence from the teams organizing the harvest of barley. The overseer gave us our instructions and told us what we would be allowed to glean, warning us to stay out of the way of the workers. We went out, and I was in the corner of the field, picking up the leftovers and scraps from the harvesting process.

It felt like a picture of my life. My entire existence was a desperate grasping at the edges of our field, hopelessly struggling to get by. Not planning or living anymore, just existing, moment to moment, day to day.

Then I saw him.

The most handsome man I had ever seen.

And the way his men responded to him! Such strength, such joy and though he was older he seemed full of vitality and youthful energy. If I could sculpt, I'd create a sculpture that would capture the essence of what I saw in him: loving power in action, masculinity moving to accomplish his goal, a focused and purposive visage in full stride surrounded by a sense of God's favor and presence.

I snapped myself out of the daydream quickly, embarrassed as if people could somehow know my thoughts. I needed to focus. Naomi was counting on me. I worked and gleaned, but truly I did little else that morning beyond stealing glances at that man.

The more I thought about it, the more depressed I became. I was a foreigner. I was poor. I was staying with Naomi, and we were destitute. I was widowed. I wasn't as young as I used to be and the worst thing of all . . . I couldn't have children.

He seemed to go out of his way to be kind and generous to all of us. I found myself at his table and he offered me food, telling me to stay with his fields and his crew through the harvest. He was probably feeling sorry for the poor widowed lady, and I tried to draw as little attention to myself as possible.

We fell back into the rhythm of working, and the coordination of the harvest team was impressive. Everyone had their job, and everyone knew their place. It was full of life, and the man who owned the field had created a place where people could belong. At some point, the workers started to sing, their steady rhythm of the scythe cutting a background to their voices. Then one voice rose above the rest, and somehow, I was not surprised when I saw whose voice it was.

His deep baritone rang out over the fields as the men sang in the afternoon sun.

At the end of the day, I had as much grain as I could carry. Naomi would be pleased; we would be okay for a few weeks at least with what I had been able to gather today.

I'll never forget the look on her face when she saw what I had gathered. She immediately began interrogating me about where I had worked, whose field had I found, who had taken notice of me. And she clapped her hands in joy at the mention of Boaz's name.

Stories of Sifted

Over the next few days something amazing happened. My heart, dead and broken in my chest, sprang to life again. My dreams of family and love and a life beyond my imagining moved back into the world of the possible.

At Naomi's instruction, I went at night to the threshing floor and lay down at the feet of my redeemer. When he awoke, he spoke gently, and I fell in love with him again.

Could it be that God could bring me back to this place? Was this restoration of everything somehow not beyond His power? This dream that I had given up on—it was being given back to me. I don't understand the workings of heaven. I don't understand the path that brought me here, or the years of sorrow we've endured.

But now I see this chance of a life with the man before me. A dream revived beyond anything I could have imagined.

> *"So, Boaz took Ruth and she became his wife. When he made love to her, the LORD enabled her to conceive, and she gave birth to a son.*
>
> *The women said to Naomi: "Praise be to the LORD, who this day has not left you without a guardian-redeemer. May he become famous throughout Israel! He will renew your life and sustain you in your old age. For your daughter-in-law, who loves you and who is better to you than seven sons, has given him birth."*
>
> *Then Naomi took the child in her arms and cared for him. The women living there said, "Naomi has a son!" And they named him Obed. He was the father of Jesse, the father of David"* (Ruth 4:13-17).

CHAPTER 4

Boaz Sifted

I remember as a boy seeing something amazing.

It was an older couple walking outside their home, framed in the cool of the day as the sun set behind them and lit the sky aflame. While older, they were still healthy and were in that wonderful time of life where the days ahead were less than the days behind, yet the days ahead were beautiful.

Walking hand in hand, they seemed so peaceful, so at rest in the love that could only be built over a lifetime of being together. At one point, they stopped, turned and looked into each other's eyes. You could see the love they shared. As they walked back to their house, having never seen me, my eyes filled with tears.

I wanted that life. I wanted it more than my next breath.

But for me, and for a love that lasts, it was never the right time.

I always dreamed of being married, of having a family and providing and protecting for them in the fullness of God's blessing. I dreamed of having my wife look at me with love and respect. Honestly, I dreamed of having the marriage all my friends seemed to have. They seemed so happy, their houses so perfect, their children so amazing.

Stories of Sifted

Being around them was an exercise in mixed emotions. I was happy for them (of course), but it hurt. My own loneliness and desire for home and family made it feel like I was at a feast that I couldn't eat of or partake in. I felt guilty that I couldn't just be glad for my friends' good fortune. I resolved to not let it get to me, trying to rejoice with them in God's blessing on their lives. How selfish could I possibly be?

That didn't work. It still hurt.

I had much to be thankful for. My land was blessed and through hard work and a good team of people, we were doing well. Even during the famine, God saw us through, and we actually increased our holding in that time. My friends would tell me to find a wife, to get out there and look.

But between my growing farming operation, taking care of my parents and the little things of life, my days were full, even if many days my heart was empty. What good is being wealthy if you don't have someone to enjoy it with?

Sifting for me was resisting the temptation to force the issue. To have my men go find a suitable mate for me and entice her with gifts and promises of wealth and the life we could have together. There was growing pressure to do this, or something similar, as I got older. Would my line continue? What was the point?

The years of waiting cost more than I can express. I felt like I was missing something important. Was my purpose really just to do well and amass wealth . . . then eventually die? Wasn't there something more? I felt called to be a father. With no marriage or prospects, that's a bit like being called to be a carpenter in a place with no trees or tools. Sometimes I questioned God and sometimes I questioned myself.

I grew older and wondered if that dream would be one that would eventually be laid to rest with the others.

My faith was expressed in simplicity. I tied my shoes. I went to work. I did the best I could. My faith was found in being loyal to my sense of things and God's working. In not trying to force the issue and make it happen on my own. In learning patience, even when that became almost too frustrating to bear. Doing the best I could and being met with success that in some ways was empty. But I was okay, and harvest was about to begin.

When she appeared.

The most beautiful girl I had ever seen.

It was like she was more real than the world around her. She was cut in relief, her colors more vibrant than the dull environment the rest of us knew. If I could paint, I would paint her. If I could write music, I would try to capture what I saw in that instant in melody and harmonic structure. People were talking to me, and I answered without really hearing them. Trying not to stare, I did little else but wonder about her throughout the morning.

I made some inquiry. She was a foreigner. She was poor. She was staying with Naomi who had returned after all these years. Ruth was a woman of character and grace who had fallen on hard times.

She came to my field. Of all the places she could have chosen, she came to me. I wondered if it was by accident or destiny. I truly didn't care as long as she came back tomorrow.

Let's see what we can do to get her to come back tomorrow.

Stories of Sifted

I don't think I've ever seen my men more amused, sharing looks and knowing glances. Love was in the air and it was catching. I surreptitiously instructed my team to help her efforts gathering a bit of leftover grain and my co-conspirators readily agreed.

The midday meal tasted better with her at the table. She turned and her hair smelled like lavender. Her easy smile came surprising, infectiously raising the hearts of those around her, like the first flower in spring. I closed my eyes and turned my face toward the sky, and the sun shone warmly on my resurrected heart. The harvesters rose and barley fell to scythes and practiced hands. The sheaves gathered and bundled in the rhythm we had known since we were children.

The men started singing in the field to pass the afternoon hours, and my voice rose to join the chorus.

It was a good day, and thanks to my men, Ruth would leave with as much food as she could carry. Naomi would get the message. We'll see where it goes from there.

Father God, is it time? Is it finally time?

Yes.

And oh, was she worth the wait.

> *"When she sat down with the harvesters, he offered her some roasted grain. She ate all she wanted and had some left over. As she got up to glean, Boaz gave orders to his men, "Let her gather among the sheaves and don't reprimand her. Even pull out some stalks for her from the bundles and leave them for her to pick up, and don't rebuke her."*
>
> *So Ruth gleaned in the field until evening. Then she threshed the barley she had gathered, and it amounted to about an ephah. She carried it*

back to town, and her mother-in-law saw how much she had gathered. Ruth also brought out and gave her what she had left over after she had eaten enough.

Her mother-in-law asked her, "Where did you glean today? Where did you work? Blessed be the man who took notice of you!" (Ruth 2:14a-19).

CHAPTER 5

Peter Sifted

Called to Follow

Mark was working on his account of Jesus' life again and asking me for stories of the time we spent with Jesus. He asked me why it was so easy for us to leave everything and follow Him.

I smiled. It wasn't easy at all. It took more than a year for me to be ready after I met Him. I had met Jesus a year before the night He called us. My fishing business was doing well. Even though I was aching for a change, that final decision to sacrifice it all was the hardest thing I'd done to that point.

Success is difficult to set aside. I had worked hard to build a life but was increasingly finding that my life and investment lacked something important. It was becoming a question of significance and legacy. I didn't want my gravestone to read, "He sold a lot of salted fish." Even so, it was comfortable, and I knew what to expect. I was longing for the risk I was afraid to say, "yes" to. Somehow, He knew my heart. I was about to be faced with the biggest choice of my life, with no guarantee that I wasn't making a huge mistake.

I drifted into memory and heard my voice recount the story to Mark of the days we became His disciples . . .

It was going to be a long night.

As the waves lifted and fell in gentle rhythm, my hands again found their resting place. The wood was worn smooth from the sheer volume of times I had touched the railing in this exact spot. I loved this time of night, even when the fish weren't moving. It was beautiful stillness. It was peace.

That was on the outside. Inside, I was boiling, desperately looking for things to change. Somehow, I knew that a new chapter was beginning, but it was frustrating to not know my next step. It was a discontent that had no anchor, no lines mooring it to anything I could point to as real.

Calling out commands to stop, our boat slowed, and I motioned for our team to throw the net. Their calloused hands, full of grace and synchronicity threw out the lines over the darkness into the sea. As it slowly fell into the deep in practiced silence, my thoughts descended too, sinking into darkness where I couldn't see.

There was nothing in my life that merited this level of unease, but I was surrounded by it nonetheless.

Is this all there is?

I had success in business, owning one of the largest fishing operations in Galilee. I spoke and dreamed and traded with partners who respected me. I ate and lived with a good family, and I had known love. I was still adrift. My life was worn smooth from the touch of years, bringing no comfort.

I wasn't in focus. Something just had to change.

We waited. So much of fishing is the waiting. The men spoke of their children in quiet tones and, like all stories of children, the exploits were completely ordinary, except to the fathers who loved them. The night stretched on as Andrew told me stories of the Baptist and the time he had spent with him these last few months.

We pulled the net for the first catch of the evening, and I murmured under my breath when it was empty. Not a single fish! That happens, but it's been years since I've seen an empty net return. I looked to the east and tried to pierce the darkness by the sheer force of my will. It didn't feel like a storm was coming.

My oldest team member barked a laugh at the dismay of the younger men and offered to let them sit and rest while he continued to work for a living. Shame isn't always a good motivator, but this time it worked pretty well. Again, I watched the practiced motions of a thousand throws, on a thousand nights, their legs and arms coiling and releasing in the carefree motion of a thousand memories, just like this one. The net flew, extended and sank for the second time.

We waited.

Andrew was telling me again about the Carpenter and the amazing things God was doing. I'd met Jesus about a year before, and I'd heard him speak. Andrew was right. There was something different about him. He spoke with a power and a love for God I'd never seen, and the stories about miracles were growing. John the Baptist was saying that he was the One. It would be perfect if Messiah came and sent the armies back to Rome. Israel was long overdue for her coming King. I would love to be a part of that revolution. That idea was exciting and scary all at the same time. I had a lot to lose.

Stories of Sifted

We pulled the nets and caught a boat full of nothing. It was time to move. We set for our second location, and I could see that the men were becoming discouraged.

Glide. Gather. Throw. Sink. Wait.

Still no fish.

The night was an empty boat, and we were getting weary. I signaled the other crew to start for shore and joked with my men as we turned to the north. One of them mentioned in passing that since the fish were smarter than we were, it was just a matter of time before they were on to us.

The earth held its breath as the sky lightened from amber to the brilliant crimson of a new day. We hit the shore, secured the boat and started unloading. Andrew cut the men loose for breakfast, sleep and time with their families. We had one more night before the Sabbath, and I set a time for us to meet again before they doggedly walked away. I told Andrew to go as well, but he just gave me that look brothers give each other before pulling a section of the first net and starting to scrape it clean.

We were still cleaning the nets when the crowd started to gather. People were buzzing about him— *Have you seen him? Is he really on his way? His teaching has such authority, I've never heard anything like this . . .* Their whispered voices slowly gained strength and echoed out over the water. I didn't see him approach, but suddenly he was there, drawing Andrew into a warm embrace. I stood and tried to wash my hands clean before greeting him, but he didn't seem to mind.

"Simon, can I use your boat to teach from?" he asked. I glanced at Andrew, who was grinning from ear to ear and of course I said yes.

It was a good idea. Sound carries over water, and as the hundreds of people who had gathered at the beach sat, Jesus began to speak.

I was exhausted, irritable and resentful of the extra time being taken. It was the worst day my business had experienced in months. I hadn't eaten, slept or bathed in far too long.

But with the Teacher in my boat, speaking God's life and love to everyone around, my heart was energized. In some small way I felt like I was a part of something significant, a partner in ministry, at least for a few moments. It felt good. I felt alive in a way I hadn't felt in years.

When he finished and dismissed the crowd, I found myself wanting him to stay but was afraid to ask if he wanted to eat with us. I wanted to impress him, to make myself important in his eyes. I wanted to let him know that I was the owner of this small fleet of ships and that our salted fish kept people fed from here to Nazareth and sometimes all the way to Egypt. As I started to take him back to shore with unspoken rehearsed words on my lips, he nodded to the south and said, "Put out into the deeper water and let down your nets for a catch."

My thoughts came quickly, almost instantaneously and were, in no particular order:

- *No.*
- *The fish aren't running this time of day.*
- *I'm tired.*
- *We just cleaned the nets; I don't want to scrape them again for nothing.*

But there was something about the way he said it and my heart was beating faster. In spite of every reason and objection I immediately replied, "We've been at this all night and haven't caught anything, but at your word, we'll cast our net again." In the corner of my eye, Andrew was nodding in approval. It seemed that whatever was happening, he felt it too.

Our weary nets spread and splashed, froze, then slowly dropped and I experienced a moment of double vision. Part of me said, "This is pointless," but another part, a deeper part, said, "Watch this!" I glanced at Andrew as the line jumped out of my hands, and I had to scramble to keep from getting pulled in. The boat lurched and dipped crazily toward the sea. Our boat was being pulled toward the net.

That's not possible.

The net was already filling. I could see the schools of fish flooding into it, just under the boat and they kept coming. When we tried to pull the catch into the boat, the net started to tear so we eased the lines back into the water to keep from losing the fish.

I called to the shore for help and they immediately launched out to help us. We pulled our second boat alongside with practiced motions to capture and load the catch. There were so many fish, both boats swamped, and we made our way carefully to the shore with a small fortune. Andrew was giving me his best, "I told you so" brotherly glance. We had more than 100 years of experience between us, and none of us had ever seen the like.

The weight of the morning continued to build until we got the boats upon the shore and I collapsed. The combination of the night's work and frustration, the path of my life and inner turmoil, the amazing words of our Teacher and the miracle we had just witnessed was too much for me to bear. This wasn't a story for other people, some rumor of God moving and doing amazing things far away. I was horribly present. God was moving nature itself to speak to me, and I suddenly felt very small.

In the very gaze of heaven, I fell to my knees. "Lord, go and leave me here, I'm full of sin and not worthy to be in your presence."

His hand on my head and his touch raising me to my feet communicated kindness and purpose. Speaking to me, to my brother, to my partners and friends, he called us to service. "Don't be afraid." And somehow, we felt peace. "From now on, you'll catch men." And we knew that it was true.

We looked at the catch, at our ravaged nets, at our boats overflowing with fortune . . . looking at the success we had worked so hard for, it was hard to walk away. But that's exactly what we did, to follow Him.

When the chance comes to leave everything else for what God calls you to do, do it—without hesitation. You'll sacrifice more than you ever imagined. You'll lose everything. You'll question that decision a thousand times but hang on with both hands to the day that He called you.

It's worth it.

> *When the disciples heard this, they were greatly astonished and asked, "Who then can be saved?" Jesus looked at them and said, "With man this is impossible, but with God all things are possible." Peter answered Him and said, "We have left everything to follow you!"* (Matthew 19:25-27).

Broken by Shame

This dream was finally over. We were about to wake up.

Stories of Sifted

Only a short time before, we had taken a short retreat to Caesarea Philippi. It's such a peaceful place, with the springs of water feeding into the Jordan and the sense of life in the land all around. We walked past the niches, with Pan and Echo singing songs over the shepherds and flocks. It was good to get away, and we took some much-needed time to rest and recharge.

Wandering among the caves and stories in relief, I wondered if men would ever carve His likeness into stone and places of worship. Would we be with Him in those images? Would my song be immortalized in art and rock, bringing glory to God for thousands of years to come? Would I be carved into the place of honor at His right Hand? It seemed within our grasp.

At one point He asked us, "Who do men say that I am?"

The answers came in a staccato beat: Elijah, John the Baptist returned, one of the prophets come back to speak over Israel again. Looking at me, He asked us directly, "Who do you say that I am?" And suddenly I knew. It was like a fire in my mind. Everything we had seen, everything we had heard came together in the thunderclap of realization. The very Word of God burning in me caused my voice to surge like a river.

You are the Christ, the Son of the Living God.

Jesus was right. It wasn't cleverness, or the available evidence that led me to believe He was the One. God Himself spoke it over all of us in an instant. There was no possibility of doubting the truth of it. And He named me. And His words were amazing.

I tell you that you are Peter, and on this rock, I will build my church and the gates of hell will not stand against it.

He was Messiah and that truth would be the foundation of the new thing He was doing. The way He said it led me to believe that I, as Peter, would also be foundational to His work. I've never felt more honored or more excited to be a part of what God was doing.

It was why I was so confused when He told us of His coming death and execution. I pulled Him aside and passionately expressed what we were all feeling; that we would never allow that to happen. He immediately chastised me, angrily calling me an enemy and stumbling block.

I was crushed by His words, wondering what all of this could mean.

There are so many things I don't understand. When we saw Him Transfigured, I knew how it was going to end.

The Son of Man would sweep aside the veil of the ordinary and people would see Him for Who He really was. He would stand before the officials and with the weight of His voice he would lower them to their knees. The high priests would understand that Messiah had come and the entire region would rise up with one voice to support Him. The nation of Israel would stand to its feet and gather around God walking among us. The pieces would fall into place quickly after that.

Fully in power, the very awe of His presence would sweep aside the Roman legions come to contain Him, and we would go in force to the capital city. Satan had tempted Him with the nations earlier on, but then the time wasn't right. God works in mysterious ways and His timing is all His own.

We were going to Rome. It was inevitable. Nothing else made any sense.

He would stand before the Senate and their money and position and power and speeches would genuflect in utter baseness before the glory

Stories of Sifted

of the One True King. He would be revealed to everyone as He was revealed to us, and it would be undeniable. They would name Him and appoint Him to rule over all the earth. A thousand years of history had paved this road to a King and Kingdom that would know no end. The *Pax Romana* was the very handiwork of God, preparing the world as a farmer prepares a field. It was so close; I could feel the earth holding its breath in anticipation. The seeds of Messiah we had planted were about to bear fruit as the world had never seen.

Jesus would be Caesar.

And He would rule the earth with justice and wisdom and the love we had come to know. The little play Emperors would tremble to speak His name aloud. The Counsels would proclaim that the Lord, He is God, and would offer sacrifices. The nations would cease to be and we would all become one people under Him. He would be divine, not just in title or idea, but in sheer, utter reality and God's chosen people would be restored to the place He had prepared for us.

The Day of the Lord the prophets had spoken of was finally here. Your kingdom come, Your will be done indeed! We would be by His side to rule and reign with Him. I would sit at His right hand, surrounded by my brothers and friends. We would share this new day with Him. We were born for this moment in time.

As you enter the city, a man carrying a jar of water will meet you. Follow Him to the house that He enters, and say to the owner of the house, "The Teacher asks: Where is the guest room, where I may eat the Passover with my disciples?" He will show you a large upper room, all furnished. Make preparations there.

We found the room exactly like He said we would. But something was wrong. Not with the preparations for Passover, but with Jesus. He wasn't acting like the time for triumph had finally come; it was more like He was about to say goodbye.

We tasted bread from His Hands and drank wine from His cup. Jesus spoke of so many things, most of them we didn't understand. He spoke of suffering and death, of kingdoms and God's perfect plan, even of our place in the coming Kingdom. He spoke of betrayal and loss and hope, and then He spoke to me.

Simon, Simon, Satan has asked to sift all of you as wheat. But I have prayed for you, Simon, that your faith may not fail. And when you have turned back, strengthen your brothers.

I boldly responded that I would never leave Him. Prison or death come what will, I was His and would never turn away. He didn't take any pleasure in telling me that I would deny Him before the next morning came. The weight of His words made me believe Him, but in spite of that, I couldn't accept it. How could I betray Him?

I resolved to do anything but that.

We only had two swords, and I claimed one of them for myself. When they came to arrest Him, I found myself looking at the moment as if it were from the outside. Time slowed down. It was time to act.

This must not be allowed to happen. Drawing the sword, I stepped in front of the Teacher and struck. I could feel my heartbeat in my ears, a pounding rhythm that felt immediately wrong. I just couldn't see any other way forward.

Jesus immediately stopped me. The sharp crack of His voice froze all of us and immediately I was ashamed. He healed the man I had struck and let Himself be arrested and taken away. I was confused, and my heart was disoriented completely. Had we misunderstood? Things couldn't end this way. The dream of our movement seemed powerless and there was a sense of dread in the air.

I followed them at a distance.

When they took Him into the house of the high priest and the men started to gather, a murmuring crowd accumulated around the fires of the courtyard. I quietly moved in among them and sat, trying to listen for anything I could gather. I could see Him, but their voices were just far enough away to be indistinct.

A servant girl tilted her head at me and motioned to her friends saying, "This one was with Him." I told them she was mistaken; I didn't know the one they called Jesus. I held my breath and prepared to run if the others didn't believe me. They looked at me without understanding and the moment passed. People came and went, whispering rumors in the chilled night air. I shifted in my cloak and made myself as small as possible, watching and listening again.

A little later someone else recognized me as well. He pointed in my direction, "You are also one of them." I replied too loudly and too forcefully that I was not. Again, others turned in interest and I felt a cold wash of fear come over me as people moved away. They didn't want to be caught up in any trouble, and it was a dark night of fear and accusation.

The proceedings continued and the Sanhedrin was deliberating, arguing back and forth, though I still couldn't hear what they said. The people around me were speculating about Him. Most seemed to think He would be imprisoned for the heresy of His teachings, perhaps He would be beaten or fined. Some time passed among the whispers before a newcomer entered our circle and with a short cynical laugh said, "Certainly this fellow was with Him, for he is a Galilean."

Chapter 5 | Peter Sifted

I vehemently denied knowing Him again and the sound that pierced my soul followed immediately after. Breathing heavily, I looked past the people and their suspicious stares, meeting the eyes of Jesus Himself. He was looking right at me. I'll never forget the sadness written in the lines of His face, half in shadow, eyes dark and hurting. He turned back to the high priest, and I ran.

Pushing past the people gathered, I ran until I couldn't run anymore, breathing, shaking and in agony. Seeking a place to hide, I sank into a shadowed corner. It wasn't supposed to end like this. A rapid flash of multiple scenes of memory surged through my mind, made poignant and vivid in my distress.

The nets that were suddenly, inexplicably full. The look on Andrew's face that communicated hope beyond measure. I saw again the blind man weeping at seeing the world for the first time. I felt the crowd gratefully taking fish and bread from my hands and buzzing about the miracle of His prayer and provision. I was surrounded again by the brightness of His glory as He spoke with Moses and Elijah.

I heard His words that pierced to my heart. I saw Him take on the Pharisees as they cowed before the weight and truth of His love. I saw Him with the children. I walked out to Him on the water. I heard His words to me earlier that evening and felt my soul tear itself into pieces, sifting like wheat, separating in ways that I couldn't possibly survive.

In my mind's eye, I denied Him again. And again. And again.

The thing that hurt the most was the cold realization that my words around the fire were true. The tears that had begun now turned into a wracking, shaking flood I couldn't hold back or stop. My denials of my Lord and my God were true. All of them were true.

Stories of Sifted

I didn't know Him at all. It was the death of a dream.

> *"Then Peter remembered the word the Lord had spoken to him: "Before the rooster crows today, you will disown me three times." And he went outside and wept bitterly"* (Luke 22:61b-62).

Restored for God's people

Joseph and Nicodemus had buried Jesus. So, when Mary came and told us what she had seen and heard, John and I raced to see for ourselves.

Was it possible? Would even death bow before my friend?

When we finally saw Him with our eyes, you've never seen a room ignite with more joy or hope. Emotionally it was a tempest, from the betrayal of my denials and guilt to the hope that He could somehow be alive again, to sadness and confusion as to where I stood. There was a lot I still didn't understand. Still, it was so good to see Him again. Everything would be okay, as long as He was with us.

Days turned into weeks and our hope grew into a sense of building expectation. Something was coming, we could feel it in our bones, but it wasn't clear what or when. I was restless and I wanted to fish. I wanted to clear my head and lose myself in the rhythm of the familiar. John and a few others decided to join me.

We didn't catch anything that night and in a private joke of fate, a figure in the distance asked if we had caught any fish. We told him we hadn't as he suggested we put our nets to the other side of the boat. It wasn't lost on any of us. We had been here before.

When the fish struck, John voiced what we were all thinking. It was Him and I was through waiting. I was all done with uncertainty and hesitation. I leapt into the cool water and swam to shore as the weight of the moment continued to build. Eating fish and bread in silence, we simply enjoyed the warmth of the morning.

When we had finished eating, He spoke to me.

"Simon son of John, do you truly love me more than these?"

The word for love He used was *agapeo*, the divine love that knows no bounds. If He had asked me, even a few days ago, I would have boldly said yes to that one. But I had stumbled, and I knew that I didn't love Him like that. My voice wavered and tears came unbidden to my eyes. Lord, you know that I love you. But it was *phileo*, the deep and authentic and cautious love of a friend.

"Feed my lambs."

Again, He said, *"Simon son of John, do you truly* agapeo *me?"*

Agapeo. I couldn't bring myself to say it back to Him. I love You as a dearest friend. I love You more than anything. But I don't love You divinely; my denial of You is proof enough. I love You, but I am painfully aware that I'm not the man You want me to be.

Jesus' response came again, *"Take care of my sheep."*

He asked a third time, *"Simon son of John, do you* phileo *me?"*

He used the word *phileo*, and it broke my heart. I don't know if it was because I wanted so badly to participate in that divine love, or if it was just the nature of affirming Him three times to unmake my threefold denial. Either way, it was the faithful wounding of a friend and not the cruel jab of revenge. God meets us where we are, to lead us where He wants us to go. So be it.

Lord, You know all things. You know that I *phileo* You.

He smiled and touched my arm, *"Feed my sheep."* And He went on to speak of things to come. His love brought me back to myself. I could feel His forgiveness and restoration. I could feel the calling of His purpose. I felt the focus of being exactly where I needed to be finally settle into my heart and mind, even my very soul.

God has called me to speak His words to this generation. I know He is with me, that He knows me better than I know myself, that He has prepared me for this time. I will speak where I was silent. I will move with Him, instead of acting impetuously on my own. I am His completely, no longer a fisherman . . . but a shepherd for His people and His presence.

It wasn't the death of a dream. It was just the beginning.

> *"Therefore let all Israel be assured of this: God has made this Jesus, whom you crucified, both Lord and Christ." When the people heard this, they were cut to the heart and said to Peter and the other apostles, "Brothers, what shall we do?"*
>
> *Peter replied, "Repent and be baptized, every one of you, in the name of Jesus Christ for the forgiveness of your sins. And you will receive the gift of the Holy Spirit. The promise is for you and your children and for all who are far off—for all whom the Lord our God will call." With many other words he warned them; and he pleaded with them, "Save yourselves from this corrupt generation."*
>
> *Those who accepted his message were baptized, and about 3,000 were added to their number that day"* (Acts 2:36-41).

CHAPTER 6

Elijah Sifted

What are you doing here, Elijah?

I'm the only one left. The work You've called me to will fail.

I've done everything You've asked. I've stood before kings to bring word of drought and economic ruin. I've called Your fire from heaven and destroyed the prophets of Baal.

We fed a widow's family. We raised a little boy from the dead.

I've prayed for rain, and You've answered. I've seen miracle after miracle. I know You are who You claim to be. But I still don't understand so many things.

This nation has turned its back on You. Your covenant lies broken. The government is twisted in evil, and your places of worship are a ruin. Your servants are dead. And in spite of Your power, I am in the wilderness running for my life and it looks like nothing has really changed.

I'm the only one left, and now they are trying to kill me, too.

Go out and stand on the mountain. I am about to pass by.

I went. Standing in wait, I closed my eyes as a tempest built around me. The wind screamed until nothing could stand before it. The swirling air focused and increased in intensity. I opened my eyes to see the very mountain before me torn apart by the force of the storm.

I was in awe of the sheer power of it. The deafening roar took on a darker, pounding shape and the distant rocks themselves began to unravel in fits and starts. They literally blasted apart from the repeated blows of furious fists of wind.

It was a storm that could sweep the earth clean of Everything. My eyes went wide at the thought that this was the end. It was too much. We had gone too far, and now the price would be paid in holy judgment. This tempest would swell and rise and flow until there was nothing left.

But the Lord was not in the wind.

It began to subside; the storm of rage and dust lost its drive and power. More quickly than I would have believed, it fell silent entirely.

I heard a rumbling as a low frequency in the distance and the ground beneath me trembled then fell still. Tilting my head to find its direction, it began again. A wave buckled the ground as far as I could see in a surreal fluid motion my eyes wouldn't accept. I waited for it to stop, for things to return to normal.

But it didn't stop. The shaking grew in violence and depth until the mountains bowed to its inimitable will. Rocks fell and were thrown, sliding crazily and resettling as pieces of the earth rose and fell like the ocean.

No kingdom could stand against this. No city, no agency, no academic ideal could withstand the wrath of the very earth itself coming to swallow them up. How small we are! We're a thin skin on the surface of the earth, easily scraped away to start fresh.

But the Lord was not in the earthquake.

I held my breath as the next wave in my lesson arrived.

It was fire.

I felt the flames before I saw them, the heat radiating in pulsing waves as it crested the horizon before me. At some point, a cool wind began to blow toward the flames, and I realized in a moment of fear that column of fire was pulling in air from the surrounding area to consume it, along with everything in its path.

Trees were consumed in seconds before a wall of fire hundreds of feet high. It charged across the side of the mountain leaving a field of ash. The flames superheated the trees and they exploded as sap became fiery pitch to spread the deathly heat in every direction. Smoke rose black and white and twisting from the fury of the red storm running.

Again, I thought, who could stand against this? Who would dare defy the One who, with a thought, could reduce a nation in glory to ash and ruin without appeal? I looked for the Lord, I listened for His voice.

But the Lord wasn't in the fire.

After the fire came a gentle whisper. I heard it and pulled my cloak around me, returning to the mouth of the cave where I had spent the night in hiding.

What are you doing here, Elijah?

I'm the only one left. My words were very much the same as my former prayer.

But this time, it was with a different voice that I answered. I was shaken by this experience, humbled by a power beyond imagining.

When God spoke again, it was with gentleness. I was to anoint kings over Aram and Israel.

And I was to finally meet my successor. The work would continue.

Most encouraging of all, I learned that I wasn't alone. Thousands in Israel still followed the Voice that whispered. God's purpose in the earth was as it should be.

The things we do consume us. Our perspective fills up our world. Like children, the hurt and fear of the moment seems like everything there is.

But it's not everything there is.

I had forgotten that our lives are threads in a tapestry in the hands of a master weaver. We're not alone in what we do, even when we are faithful and discouraged and the path is hard to see.

Our effect on generations to come is measured by the One who walks upon the wind, Whose very presence causes the mountains to tremble and whose heart is an all-consuming fire. Look beyond the enemies. Know that God is mighty beyond anything we've ever dreamed.

I learned that often He chooses to work, not through a show of power, but through a whisper to a human heart. The hope that I found wasn't in strength to move mountains but in the knowledge that I wasn't alone.

We are part of something bigger and God's plan is a good one. What discouragement could stand in the face of such love?

"The Lord heard Elijah's cry, and the boy's life returned to him, and he lived. Elijah picked up the child and carried him down from the room into the house. He gave him to his mother and said, "Look, your son is alive!"

Then the woman said to Elijah, "Now I know that you are a man of God and that the Word of the Lord from your mouth is the truth" (I Kings 17: 22-24).

CHAPTER 7

Hosea Sifted

I didn't want her back.

I was angry and doubly so at the thought that I should have known better. A leopard doesn't change its spots. Why would I expect someone like her to suddenly be faithful because of a promise? All of her vows were just words and empty air, carrying no weight that would ever make a difference in the heart. On second thought, I have no doubt that she meant every word she said, just not for very long. That makes it worse, not better.

She left of her own free will. Let her own the consequences of her mistakes. Let her new situation take care of her, or leave her to die, I don't care which. It will sound funny, but I've never been tempted by murder before. It always seemed so unthinkable and so far away. But I wanted to hurt the ones who had hurt me. I wanted them to pay.

I wanted her to pay.

That lasted for a few days, until I remembered God's word to me. Our marriage was a picture of God's relationship with Israel. Our children were named according to His moving. I was reminded that my part in our marriage was to love her as best I could. And while our marriage being healthy and good was dependent on both of us playing our parts well, my love for her was not based on what she did or didn't do.

I loved her, simply because she was mine.

And my expression of love was not dependent on her response, or faithfulness, or willingness to change or get it right. My love for her was simply my love for her, seeing the best in her, seeing who she could be.

Don't misunderstand. Our marriage was absolutely dependent on her being willing to be married, with all that entailed. You can't have a marriage with only one person involved. But my part of the picture was mine alone . . . and ultimately that is what God has called me to.

I wondered how God must feel as we are faithless toward Him. How we are distracted by the whim and pleasure of the moment, forgetting Him completely. I suddenly experienced a sort of double vision. My anger, disappointment and love juxtaposed with His anger, disappointment and love for her—and for all of Israel.

I felt His disappointment and love even for me. I wasn't the man I needed to be either. I was as faithless as she was toward heaven in many cases and I fell to my knees in repentance, asking God to bring me back to Himself.

My anger changed from being angry at her betrayal of me, to being angry at the situation she was now trapped within. It was a story that cut her off from her true potential: being beautiful before God and walking in a life of purity and contentment.

The price I paid for her was nothing compared to the price He paid for me. It was nothing compared to the price He paid for Israel. It was nothing compared to the price He would be willing to pay to redeem the whole earth back to Himself. My heart beating faster, I decided it was time to act.

When I finally found her, she was broken. She was ashamed and had less than nothing. As I bought her out of the slavery, she had sold herself into, the look in her eyes was mixed with fear and sorrow and frustration and disbelief—and hope. She knew she didn't deserve a second chance, and she wept at the realization that this wasn't about what she deserved.

It was about what I was willing to give.

My words over her were God's words and I took my wife home to heal, to rest, to love and to do everything I could to mend the wounds our house had borne. It was a long path, and it took years before we would have a relationship that either one of us would call blessed. But we will get there. With God's help, we will.

In my heart I knew that His will and power would be made known and that things would eventually change for the better. That before I died, I would know the love and marriage I longed to possess and be a part of. I knew that I would be able to say in truth that I wouldn't trade her for anything. I knew that I would express my love to her with all of my heart. I knew that she was faithful and pure, a great mother to our children and a blessing for generations to come.

It cost me everything. And I would pay that price again without hesitation.

God's heart to us is the same. Come back to Him when He calls.

> "The Lord said to me, "Go, show your love to your wife again, though she is loved by another and is an adulteress. Love her, as the Lord loves

the Israelites, though they turn to other gods and love the sacred raisin cakes.

So, I bought her for fifteen shekels of silver and about a homer and lethek of barley. Then I told her, "You are to live with me many days; you must not be a prostitute or be intimate with any man, and I will live with you" (Hosea 3:1-3).

CHAPTER 8

Job Sifted

I t all happened so fast. Report after report of catastrophe came to me in a series of events that defied belief. I was in shock for days trying to accept the magnitude of my world crashing in around me.

I buried my wife and children on a beautiful spring day as creation held its breath in response to my grief. Sprinkling flowers on the earth where they lay, I offered an angry prayer to heaven, asking God to keep them. Asking Him to take me, too.

My fortune was gone. My family was gone. Finally, even my health and physical body were gone.

I sat in sackcloth and ashes, broken and beyond comfort. And like everyone who has ever suffered, I asked why. What did this mean? It didn't make any sense, and I needed it to. In the night of great distress, these questions aren't interesting exercises in logic and philosophy; they are all we have left and their weight and import magnifies beyond imagining.

My friends and I wrestled with those questions. We framed them and tried to bend them to our will, making sense of this world around us. The disconnect between what I know in my heart to be true and my undeniable experience of the world around me is like a splintering of the mind. It hurts. It doesn't work. The failure to master these things leads to despair, and I was all the way there.

My *counselors* argued that I had sinned, though I knew I had not. They spoke eloquently and fashioned beautiful constructs of logic. I must have done something to deserve it; God is not capricious in allowing bad things to happen. They were masterful. They were passionate. They were polished in philosophy and presentation.

They were wrong.

The answer came, fittingly enough, not from answers, but from questions. Questions from God Himself and the terrible, intimate, inescapable weight of His presence.

Where were you when I laid the earth's foundation?

Who shut up the sea behind doors when it burst forth from the womb?

Have you ever given orders to the morning, or shown the dawn its place?

On the face of it, those things might seem harsh, as if God were setting me down hard and humbling me. But it was different than that. It was an experience filled with glory and with love. He spoke to me in a way that I could understand, and I needed His words more than I have ever needed anything.

And all of His questions had answers: I was nowhere. You did. I have not.

And those answers set me free in His presence. They placed me in a world where I could rejoice and trust in His power. I was not adrift. I was not beyond His reach. I was on a sea where God is my captain and able to complete what He has considered. The tempest of His storm wasn't for my destruction, but for my shaping.

The pain of the moment is here, but then it is gone, giving way to the next moment of experience or sense. The only thing that remains is our response to it. Our dread of the coming moment, our fear and horror of the present tragedy, our poignant memory of the slice of time . . . that is what becomes part of our soul.

As individuals, only our internal framing of meaning is eternal. Only our response to the world is forever.

That's why forgiveness is so important. And why love is critical. It's God's way for us to remake and participate rightly in our experience of the world around us. It's why trusting in heaven to come isn't just a copout or a rhetorical shell game.

So, don't misunderstand what is really happening when you suffer.

It isn't an unbearable sequence of events that God is using to punish you. It isn't the deception of a universe that appears to be kind, suddenly exposed as cruel. It isn't the test of standing firm in the face of hopelessness in the way that you might think.

It's an opportunity to alter your soul. It's a chance to be remade again in the image and glory of God, responding in a way that will bless you (and everyone you meet), forever.

I wish I could take your heart into my heart.

I wish I could show you how wonderful it feels to let go and trust in the author of creation beyond the pain of the moment. I wish I could bring you to the place I've found, where the voice of God brings surety and comfort beyond any other.

The solution to the problem of pain isn't a beautiful argument. The best thought, the best argument, the best realization . . .

. . . is the presence of God Himself.

> *"You said, "Listen now and I will speak: I will question you, and you shall answer me." My ears had heard of you, but now my eyes have seen you. Therefore I despise myself and repent in dust and ashes"* (Job 42:4-6).

CHAPTER 9

Paul Sifted

Three days is a long time to be in darkness.

It's long enough to think about what you've done. It's long enough to reflect on how wrong you've been. It's long enough to realize that you've participated in murder. It's long enough to consider how much of an enemy of God you really are.

It's also long enough for your other senses to sharpen in compensation. I experienced deeply the clinking of utensils used to prepare food. I felt the way the sound of a room changes when a door is opened. I heard things I don't ever remember hearing before, and I gathered the world around me through smell and changes in the movement of the air. It was a time of heightened sense both externally and internally. My introspection went deep and was relentless in nature.

The bright light that flashed around me was just the beginning. Knocking me from my path to the ground, it was a literal shock—a small thing compared to the spiritual earthquakes to come.

In my crusade against the Way, I had never once considered it might actually be true. I hadn't wrestled with the possibility that Messiah had actually come and walked among us. I hadn't seen Stephen as he truly

Stories of Sifted

was, a holy and great man, not a crazed and raving heretical cancer. I was the one who was lost. My heart was the true cancer, and it was being excised hour by hour in unseen extremis and pain.

In my blindness, I saw Isaiah for the first time. And trembling, I realized the promise of Abraham had come. Scripture after scripture seared my thoughts with fire, and I simply couldn't believe I hadn't seen all this before. He came from Bethlehem. He was from the house of David. The signs I discounted as fanciful rumors and wish fulfillment were real. Of course, He was the one. How could I have missed this? How could anyone miss this?

And He was opening a door beyond the captive children of Israel. This was for all nations. Everything I knew before was becoming unknown . . . and my hands gripped the rough cloth around me as revelation swirled like the rain.

I felt gentle hands and voices as they offered me food and drink, but I refused. I couldn't eat yet, this was too important. I didn't want anything to break the spell of this realization until it was time.

The Christ had come. His Spirit would be poured out on all flesh. And I would get to be a small part of His working in these early days. I would speak over cities, I would write things to be revealed.

When Ananias came, I was ready. I was drinking deeply of His presence and while excited, I was more than a little afraid of what would happen next. Still, I was ready. His voice to me was as clear as music confirming what I already knew in my heart. As he prayed, I felt the weight of my old life break away and I gasped as my eyesight returned.

In joy, I held my breath as his hands lowered me into the water. Closing my eyes, I was returning to the horrible, blessed darkness that had been my world for a time. A heartbeat, two, and then a gentle pulling led me back into the light. Rising from the water into the sweet air of redemption, I was surrounded by men whose hearts were full of love for me. I embraced every one of them and they didn't seem to mind getting a little wet from the waters of my resurrection.

We ate together and talked of many things as I took my first communion with them at the table. God's presence was as thick as incense on high holy days, a powerful context for a simple meal. I felt alive. I felt amazing. My mind continued to roll, and everything pointed to Him.

I was born again.

When this story is told, the focus will inevitably be on the divine light and dramatic nature of the moment. Men will recall the very voice of God thundering to me upon the road. I'm not downplaying that; and the truth is, I'm ashamed that it took such extreme measures to get my attention. The more poignant lesson for me was this:

Love one another.

It was my first lesson of true spiritual life. I experienced it from the ones who helped me walk, leading me to safety. I learned it as others cared for me, unable to feed or care for myself in basic ways. I saw the heart that God Himself had placed in His people and saw their willingness to play their part. And I learned the greatness of His love, not from loving, but from being loved. In my weakness, He showed His great love through the very people I sought to destroy.

God's plan is bigger than ours. His powerful love can cause a movement bigger than anything we could start or catalyze. Close your eyes. Surrender. Start at the beginning. And . . .

Love one another.

> *"Saul spent several days with the disciples in Damascus. At once, he began to preach in the synagogues that Jesus is the Son of God. All those who heard him were astonished and asked, "Isn't he the man who raised havoc in Jerusalem among those who call on this name? And hasn't he come here to take them as prisoners to the chief priests?"*
>
> *Yet Saul grew more and more powerful and baffled the Jews living in Damascus by proving that Jesus is the Messiah"* (Acts 9:19b-22).

PERSONAL CHARACTER

CHAPTER 10

Adam Sifted

The rules we set down for our children are for their good and protection. Love writes those rules and following them brings a blessing that lasts forever.

It's a simple truth: Obeying God's heart for us brings good things; disobeying brings tragedy and separation.

I remember those days with a relaxed mixture of joy and contentment, for the days spent in simple pleasure were heavenly. I remember the first time I felt sunshine on my face turned up to the sky so warm and welcoming. I remember feeling the dew beneath my feet in the amber-covered mornings. I can taste the sweetness of the fruit God provided us. I can smell Eve's hair in the embrace she freely gave, secure in the knowledge that we were literally made to be together.

Walking with the Ancient of Days in the evening are the memories I cherish most. Telling Him all about the things we did, the names we had created for the ones in our care. It was a wonderful sharing of the discovery of creation and the new experiences we had known. I could feel His pleasure in us.

Stories of Sifted

A part of me is glad my children and children's children never saw the Garden. I think they would be less joyful if they really understood how far we have fallen. For me, it's a reality I can't escape and the passing years don't lessen the burden I bear. I love Eve. I love my family. In that sense, this life has been good, in spite of the curse and guilt I feel for separating future generations from the life we knew. We've eaten and the little ones want to hear about the Garden again.

Though it hurts in the telling, they will hear it again. Remembering that place still makes me pause and brings tears to my soul. Is there a heavier-borne remorse than a king without a kingdom? How can I convey the difference of life now compared to what we knew?

We lost our Home.

The accounts of our story to future generations will mention that Eve was deceived as she was tempted. But the story will not talk about my misunderstanding or the idea that I was deceived.

That's because I wasn't deceived.

I didn't try to stop her. I was tempted, too. I wanted to know the things I didn't know. I wanted to be more than I was. But when she bit into the forbidden, I was suddenly aware of where we were, and the weight of the moment hit me fully. It was a slice of time filled with possibility and the metallic taste of fear was in my mouth.

I had lost her. She looked at me with a new awareness and fear filled her eyes. The terror and shame and insight combined in a way she never expected or wanted, and the serpent was looking, not at her but at me. His hungry, expectant eyes knew he had me even before I took the fruit myself. Do I turn away from her? Or from God?

Chapter 10 | Adam Sifted

I knew the price I would pay when I tasted the fruit. I betrayed God and disobeyed Him willingly, with my eyes wide open. Both of us sinned striving for something good, but we disobeyed the One who gave us everything for our own selfish ends. Eve desired to be more like the Father we loved. For me, I did not want to lose her. I did not want her to face the horrible consequences alone. By lifting my desire and relationship for her above my relationship with God, I condemned us both.

Trying to accomplish something good through illegitimate means will never work in the end. Turning our backs on God always makes things worse and separates us from who we truly are.

I tell our story as an explanation, to help the coming generations understand why there is evil in the world. Why are we the way we are? Where did we come from? Why are there things in our lives that are so hard to bear and understand?

I tell our story as a warning, to help them learn from our mistakes. If we weep at the part we played in our separation from God, let that be a lesson to carry the weight of warning to them deeply and well.

I tell our story as a promise, to bring generations hope. God loves us and will make a way for us to recapture everything we've lost. Even in the story of our fall, there are seeds of hope and hints of the redemption to come.

The very deepest part of me, even my *bones* remember walking in the cool of the day with Him. Deep within you, somehow, you remember that day, too. It's why you long for a time when you will walk with Him again. The path to that day is not closed. It is a dream that will be fulfilled.

The rules He sets down for us, His children, are for our good and protection. Love writes those rules and following them brings a blessing that lasts forever. If you hear anything from me, hear this—a simple truth.

Obeying God's heart for you brings good things. Disobeying brings tragedy and brokenness. Take the better road.

You'll never regret it.

> *"When the woman saw that the fruit of the tree was good for food and pleasing to the eye, and also desirable for gaining wisdom, she took some and ate it. She also gave some to her husband, who was with her, and he ate it.*
>
> *Then the eyes of both of them were opened, and they realized they were naked; so they sewed fig leaves together and made coverings for themselves. Then the man and his wife heard the sound of the LORD God as he was walking in the garden in the cool of the day, and they hid from the LORD God among the trees of the garden. But the LORD God called to the man, "Where are you?"* (Genesis 3:6-8).

CHAPTER 11

Abraham Sifted

I married Sarai in the land of my father, a place called Ur, before God called us to go. Looking back, it seems odd that we didn't know where we were going. I do remember the move feeling right, beyond reason or explanation. She felt it too, so we went. Our sense of purpose was clear, and it was easy to trust.

My bones are older now, and she is gone. Looking over the canvas of my days, I remember divine moments and conversations, and I see that God is so faithful in every single thing He promised. His words to me as a young man are finding their beginning in the earth. I can see in my children the nations they will become. Their children will be generations upon generations held in the very hands of God.

I can still hear His voice to me like it was yesterday.

Your children will be like the stars in the sky.

And it's happening. I don't deserve how good God has been to me.

Yet sometimes I wonder about the mistakes I've made. There are so many things I would undo if I could.

When I convinced Sarah to lie about being my wife to the Egyptians, it seemed so necessary. The famine was severe; both of us were very afraid. She was immediately noticed like I knew she would be. Pharaoh treated me extremely well for her sake, like I knew he would. I've never been more frustrated for being right.

My decision put her in an impossible situation and wounded her deeply. More than that, it wounded "us" deeply. She still loved me. I still loved her.

But our relationship was never quite the same.

Seasons came and went, but the years of trying and remaining childless were the hardest. To watch the joy and growth of children, who are not your own, is bittersweet.

Our hope for a son by itself was a strong one. Coupled with God's words about our destiny, it was unbearable. We were failing Him. The dream of starting a nation to bless the earth eventually was something we just didn't talk about. For years we lived just maintaining our house and wealth. The hope of children faded like a barely remembered dream.

When we were older and the chance for our own children was long past, we came up with a plan to return to the dream God had for us. Sarah suggested Hagar, and it seemed like a way for us to finally have the children we longed for. It seems obvious now, but I could have said, "No."

I dishonored my wife completely. I was trying to do what I felt was right, what I talked myself into believing God would have me do to carry on our family name and heritage. I was such a fool.

It's a hard lesson, but if we trust God to do only the things we can do without Him, that isn't trusting at all. That's glorifying our own effort and calling it divine.

It wasn't until God spoke that the weight of our mistake settled on my heart completely. I looked at my hands, now grown old. I looked at my wife's features and her beautiful gray hair, seeing for the first time what I had missed all of these years.

God wasn't bringing the promise through me.

He was bringing the promise through *us*.

His plan was for Sarah to make this journey with me. He changed her name, too.

The times I trusted God afterward—the great moments of faith and the stories that live on—all find their root in the failures I experienced with her. The fear, the lack of trust and the belief that the promise was dependent on us were all revealed in my relationship with Sarah.

He used my mistakes and lack of courage to open my own heart to me. He used those moments to teach me and to lead me closer to Him. But the wounding she experienced wasn't the only way for God to shape me; it was the path that I chose. I would do that differently if I could.

All of my regrets find a single truth in common: I didn't love Sarah like I should have.

So, focused on what I wanted God to do, I lost so much of the joy that we should have had together. The way I pursued my work and my drive to follow God hurt my marriage. My wife paid a heavy price to walk through life with me.

"Then Abraham breathed his last and died at a good old age, an old man and full of years; and he was gathered to his people. His sons Isaac and Ishmael buried him in the cave of Machpelah near Mamre . . . the field Abraham had bought from the Hittites.

There, Abraham was buried with his wife Sarah" (Genesis 25:8-10).

CHAPTER 12

Isaac Sifted

When you're young, no one tells you what it's like to be old.

The most alarming thing is how much pain you experience on a daily basis. Your days are filled with a backdrop of little pains and larger pains, from old injuries and the stress of life compounded by your strength now slowly fading. The pain of the soul can add up as well. For God doesn't see as we do and sometimes He works His will despite our intention and the misunderstanding of His plan. Blessed be the Lord, whose grace is not limited by the shortsighted vision of blind old men.

I would have chosen Esau.

That fateful morning, I woke in a horrible mood, back and legs aching and from a night that was far from restful. My dim eyes were failing (like the rest of me), and I needed to pass our family legacy to my son. We were called to be a nation, increasing in power and influence until all the world would be blessed through us. It was a weighty burden I had inherited from my father. My son would inherit it from me. It was time to pass this torch to the next generation and wait for my final rest to come.

Stories of Sifted

Calling Esau into my room, I asked him to hunt and prepare a feast to honor the occasion. Though my appetite was fading, I wanted to experience a moment of good life again. I longed to sit before the freshly prepared meal that was the result of a day spent hunting. I wanted to recapture a moment of youth through memory and the prowess of my favorite son. He readily agreed, not realizing the weight of what I was asking.

The early part of our day waned, and I napped a bit before hearing him return.

The aroma of the meal was wonderful, but as we spoke something was amiss. Esau was never one to be talkative, but he seemed even more reticent than usual. My eyes only able to make out the shape of him, I asked him to come near and allow me to touch him . . . and he did. With my son before me, I felt the Spirit of God moving and the blessing rose from my heart into the late morning air:

Ah, the smell of my son is like the smell of a field the Lord has blessed. May God give you of heaven's dew and of earth's richness an abundance of grain and new wine.

May nations serve you and peoples bow down to you. Be lord over your brothers and may the sons of your mother bow down to you. May those who curse you be cursed and those who bless you be blessed.

It was only later that I learned how I had been deceived.

I was furious, but even in the midst of emotion and realization I knew God was at work. He was turning me even as it was happening. Even in anger, I knew the blessing to Jacob must remain given. I hated this. And the same time, I was grateful that sometimes God uses us in spite of ourselves.

It wasn't right what Jacob did. He will pay a high price for his choices. But his desire was for the blessing of God and his heart was after the things that heaven wanted. It doesn't excuse his deception, but I was blind in my own planning and preferences, instead of seeking what God was doing. Jacob was a prince, and the dimness of my vision wasn't just physical.

I was looking as men do, at the strength we can easily see. In contrast, God sees clearly, looking at the heart and honoring those who seek Him with everything. It's humbling when your own schemes are frustrated because you didn't discern God's working. It's a bitter thing to know that there are times when He works around you, instead of through you. It isn't easy, but have the character to admit you are wrong and move back into step with Him.

Trust God. Trust in His genius. Trust Him more than your own senses or ability to plan. Be flexible when He upends your strategy unexpectedly and change to meet His course.

You'll find a blessing that expands to generations.

> *"May God Almighty bless you and make you fruitful and increase your numbers until you become a community of peoples. May He give you and your descendants the blessing given to Abraham . . ."* (A Blessing from Isaac to Jacob, Genesis 28:3-4a).

CHAPTER 13

Jacob Sifted

I always had an angle.

My gift was cleverness, and I used it to full advantage. Even my name meant, "to grasp" and grasp I did. From my brother's heel at birth to our competitiveness as children, I was always reaching for more. I was never content, always looking for a way to win. Encounters were never what they appeared to be. I was lurking in a constant undercurrent of planning and scheming to further my own interests.

I never had a conversation without an agenda. I never did anything unless it benefited me directly. It was manipulative, but that was the way of the world. I wasn't strong like my brother; I had to find my own strength in unexpected ways.

With Esau, that was surprisingly easy; he was a man of passion and lived entirely for the moment. When I tricked his birthright from him with a bowl of soup, I played on his hunger and weakness. I took advantage of his simple nature and robbed him of things beyond his ability to apprehend.

Stories of Sifted

It even worked with our father, Isaac, as I deceived him in his blindness and old age into blessing me above my brother. I wanted that blessing, and I was willing to do anything to get it.

Lie. Cheat. Steal. Scheme. It was evil and I knew it.

Eventually, my deceptive lines came back to steal years of my life. Laban had used my own trick to press Leah into my family. He let me think I was entering into covenant with the one that I loved, but instead finding my pledge was made to deception. I deserved that one. It was poetic justice for my own choices, and my second seven years of labor were bitter ones.

Now it had all come to an end. Esau was about to cross my path again, and I was all out of ideas. I tried to prepare the way with gifts and bribes to soften him toward me, but it was no use. He was coming in force to meet me, and I was terrified at what he would do to my family. Esau wasn't subtle. The message of the men coming with him wasn't lost on me.

I was broken and I was done. I divided us into groups, hoping my death would buy time for at least some of my children to escape. It was time to pay the price and ultimately, I would find myself at his mercy. With no other choice, I cried out to God. And I meant it.

It was in the dead of night, hours before I was to meet my brother again.

A man who was not a man met me and we wrestled. There was no time for talk. There was no room for clever schemes or prepared deception. We fought and I could find no advantage. There was no insight; no measured words of diplomacy or charm, and all my weapons were stripped away to sweat and desperation. There was no agenda, only the moment. And I threw myself headlong into pure struggle.

It was the most honest moment of my life.

Minutes turned into hours as the spiritual weight of the moment crushed my heart into dust. The uncertainty of my fate at the strong, heavy hands of my brother had left me weary to the point of exhaustion. The man kept coming, and nothing I did could fend him off.

Then he touched my hip and I buckled. I literally felt the internal working of my bone and sinew wrench violently out of place. It felt like unraveling and my vision went white with the effort, but I held on. I held until the whole world faded into a single purpose and everything else faded away. I was not giving up, no matter what.

And just like that, it was over. I knew I was in the presence of God.

Filled with power, he spoke to me a blessing and gave me my true name. As the day broke into light, I was born again. The grasping and dishonesty of my old life faded with the dew. I named the place Face of God, for I had met Him and in His presence He spared my life.

When I went out to meet Esau, I met him with a limp.

He had forgiven me for the things I had done. Oddly, it was good to see my brother. It was good to put that chapter of my life to rest in resolution.

My life was different after that and I strove to be a man worthy of the name He had given. Those days of sifting left a mark on my soul and a change in my ability to walk as a reminder. The lesson was simple, but

Stories of Sifted

it took me a lifetime to learn: Desperately grasp onto the blessing of God, in humility, in integrity and in the fullness of His truth.

My real inheritance and my true name came not through scheming but through perseverance and simple faith that hangs on even when it hurts.

> *"But Jacob replied, "I will not let you go unless you bless me." The man asked him, "What is your name?" "Jacob," he answered.*
>
> *Then the man said, "Your name will no longer be Jacob, but Israel, because you have struggled with God and with men and have overcome"* (Genesis 32:26b-28).

CHAPTER 14

Joseph Sifted

I had to leave the room.

I was overcome with emotion; so many years of wounding that I thought I had dealt with were coming back in force. It was too much. I was awash in a flood of simultaneous feelings: anger, hope, relief, hurt, love and the idea that God was bringing things back together for my healing. It simply overwhelmed me.

I came from a mixed family. My father had children with multiple wives, and, like many such situations, this caused a lot of problems and dysfunction. I was talented, even as a kid, and that delighted my parents. My father expressed that delight with favor and expensive gifts. He made it clear that he liked me better than my brothers, and as you can imagine, my brothers just "loved" that about me. To make matters worse, I flaunted my status with them and took every opportunity to rub their noses in it.

That eventually caused a rift that went farther than I ever imagined. Human trafficking became the measured and reasonable response that saved me from being murdered. I was sold as a slave, and through a series of events, I ended up in prison before God eventually pulled me out.

The building of our character and our family's dysfunction are horribly intertwined in our early formation. Success, no matter how poignant or expansive, means little without resolving childhood wounding.

It had been years since I had considered how much this is true. The days in prison left me a lot of time for reflection and contemplation of my family and early life.

Now, my brothers were waiting for my response and were very much afraid. They didn't recognize the arrogant child they had done away with.

If they had, they would have been terrified.

I had dreamed of this moment as a boy, sold into slavery. In prison, I had dreamed of what I would say and do if I ever had a chance to face them again. The speech I had rehearsed a thousand times seemed small to me now. I never thought I would give it while holding their lives in my hands. I was in a different place. They didn't know the agony of soul I had experienced in forgiving them years ago.

When I reveal my name to them, I wonder if they will expect the worst? If they are afraid of retribution, so be it. They had earned a bit of fear. My coat of many colors had acquired an ugly red stain at the end of my chapter with them. Let that horrible crimson and the pattern of blood splattered with lies fill their vision for the day.

And yet, I would try to bring healing, even here. I would feed them and bring their families into my house. I would hold the hands of my father again and feel the weight of his embrace.

For I had found bread in the very dreams of God, and my word held the favor of the king of kings. My sons were favorites at court and doing well. Promoted from son to slave to criminal to national leader, I knew that God was very much in control. But after all these years, would father know me? How would he remember the son who was lost? Could the relationship with my brothers know redemption beyond the writing off of a very bad debt? Did God provide for even this moment in His sequence of dreams and plans for me?

With the vision of the child night, the sun and stars and moon, they bowed. And the colors of my heart had taken on the favor of my heavenly Father, replacing the coat I had lost so many years before. The series of events had led me into God's plan beyond my brothers' ill intent, to the place where I held provision for nations. I re-entered the room and held them with my gaze.

It was time.

I am Joseph, the one you sold into a life of slavery beyond appeal or reprieve so many years ago.

Things moved quickly after that.

We don't get to choose our family or early life. We don't get to choose the mistakes of our parents. We don't get to choose the abuse of siblings, or the things done that can never be undone. But if God orchestrates our context before the beginning of time, then His purpose can be seen even there. We don't meet Him in an empty room. We meet Him in this place, crafted by a divine dream to mold us according to His will.

It is a mystery that we don't understand these things until later in life, if we ever really do. But we do get to choose how we respond. We get to choose the shape and purpose of our heart. We do get to finally be free.

Family dysfunction is an opportunity for God to do amazing things. Not just for me personally, but for thousands upon thousands of generations to come. My family of origin is the first and last place I've learned to forgive. That lesson has led to the best dream of all.

> *"And now do not be distressed or angry with yourselves because you sold me here, for God sent me before you to preserve life. For the famine has been in the land these two years, and there are yet five years in which there will be neither plowing nor harvest.*
>
> *And God sent me before you to preserve for you a remnant on earth, and to keep alive for you many survivors. So it was not you who sent me here, but God. He has made me a father to Pharaoh, and lord of all His house and ruler over all the land of Egypt"* (Genesis 45:5-8).

CHAPTER 15

Moses Sifted

A prince in the house of the most powerful ruler on earth, I was surrounded by wealth. Even my toys were made by artisans. I studied history, philosophy, medicine, language and strategies of war as part of my education in the court of Egypt. I was a favorite among Pharaoh's family.

When I made the transition to my true people, the Hebrews, I led them with grace and the undeniable power of God. My calling at the burning bush and the plagues of Egypt led us to exodus and the freedom of the nation of God's people. The parting of the Red Sea gave us a sense of purpose and destiny, and nothing seemed impossible with heaven on our side.

With a pillar of cloud by day and fire by night, I led our people for a generation. We were fed with manna and walked according to His law, which I received from God Himself on the mountain. We built the ark of the covenant, the tabernacle of His presence and while He prepared us in the desert, I wrote the first five books of holy Scripture. I helped shape and prepare Joshua to be my successor. It was an amazing time of God's leading and blessing in spite of our shortcomings. I was honored to be a leader for this time in our story.

But before that, I was sifted.

Before I was a leader, I was a murderer.

Passionate about justice, I had lobbied for the Hebrews to be treated well. It wasn't just that I was secretly one of them. As leaders, we had a responsibility to our people, to make their lives better and lead them to be part of a great nation. But many saw the Hebrews as a simple tool to be used up and discarded. They were, to some, a means to the end of the Great Pyramids and, honestly, not much more than that.

When I saw the overseer beating that Hebrew man, the action became everything that was wrong in the world all at once. The movement from thought to consideration to action all happened in a fluid line unbroken in my heart. When I acted, it was with icy precision and weighted, deliberate blows. I took everything he had and everything he ever would have in a moment. I did it with the intent to kill him.

Then I buried him in the sand.

Eventually, word of my actions spread, and I was running for my life. Even Pharaoh had issued a death warrant for the crime. I fled Egypt, thinking I'd never return. I was promoted from prince to shepherd for my anger and lived that life mixed with the unbalanced feelings of guilt, unease, contentment and regret for almost 40 years.

God was faithful in His love for me, though my crime haunted me the rest of my life.

When He called me at the burning bush, I was murdering the Egyptian again in my mind. How could He use a man like me to lead? When we were fleeing and trapped before the Red Sea, I was wondering if my sin had doomed us all.

When I received the commandment "Thou shalt not kill," it was written in stone and tears.

And when I became angry and struck the rock for water, it wasn't about the moment of frustration. It was about the man I had been so many years ago. I was turning away from the life God had borne in me, back to a time when I acted on my own impulsive passion. I had tried to help God's people in my own way. That path was disaster for me, and looming disaster for the ones I serve.

In God's Hands and in His purpose, we're not defined by our mistakes. But He uses our repentance to shape us in ways I never would have imagined.

His will caused even my greatest character failings to lead me to His grace. He can use even our greatest regrets to teach and shape us into the people He wants us to be.

Look to God. Let your failures lead you to compassion and meekness in leadership. Let your weakness be a wall against pride and a reason to depend on Him even more.

> *"And God said, "I will be with you. And this will be the sign to you that it is I who have sent you: When you have brought the people out of Egypt, you will worship God on this mountain"* (Exodus 3:12).

CHAPTER 16

Samson Sifted

I woke to the laughter of my enemies.

Blinking, I looked to my left and to my right. It was dark, with the flickering light of torches in the distance casting mocking shadows on the wall before me. My shoulders hurt from the awkward weight of my position. I pulled my feet underneath me and slowly stood.

I was underground. My hands were bound at the wrist by thick bronze chains leading to the stone behind me. My feet were restricted in similar fashion; the heavy chains made soft noises as they resisted my adjusted stance. I swung my right hand in a quick circle and felt the bronze links in my hand. I did the same with my left.

Rolling my neck and shoulders, I pulled myself a shuffling step forward, until the chains binding me went taut. My restraints were about to become my weapons. Their laughter would die with cries of terror and surprise soon enough. Taking a deep breath, I flexed against the chains to pull them free of their stone housings.

Nothing happened.

Growling, I reset and stepped forward again, losing my balance and jerking myself upright. The muscles in my arms and chest flexed as I shook my head to feel my hair around me. Something was wrong. I tilted my head to the left and rubbed my ear and scalp on my shoulder. I could feel the rough remaining tufts of stubble on my skin. My hair was gone. The symbol of my vow had been cut away completely. I was betrayed.

Panicked, I pulled at the chains desperately. Wide-eyed and straining I began to tremble in futile effort. It was no use. God had abandoned me. My strength was gone, replaced by cold anger. I didn't deserve this. I would make them pay.

I would make her pay.

Someone was coming, several someones from the sound of it. They rounded the corner of the passage before me and were carrying several items I didn't recognize. A large metal pot with a heavy handle, glowing with red-hot coals, swung slowly between the two soldiers carrying it. A makeshift table with blocks and straps was being carried as well, but it was too tall to be a table, I didn't know its purpose. A smallish man carrying a scroll was reading in a monotone; it sounded like he was reading a list of names. I cursed them all soundly.

The soldiers set the coals on the ground to my right. The table carrier brought the apparatus directly in front of me and set it down. I tried to grab him, but the heavy chains combined with my exhaustion made me easy to avoid. Even so, it took three of them to manhandle me on top of the table. They adjusted the straps and blocks to hold my head in place. I was still chained to the wall, and I just couldn't get enough leverage to resist. The small man was still reading names, one after the other.

From the corner of my eye, I saw the lead soldier put a sharpened length of bronze into the coals and over time, it started to glow with

Chapter 16 | Samson Sifted

the heat from the surrounding material. At some point, I realized the names were names of Philistine families.

They were the names of the men I had killed.

It took hours to read them all.

When his voice finally droned away into silence, I was in agony. My back cramped from the unnatural position. My arms and legs were still chained, and I couldn't straighten or move my head. The small man handed his scroll to a soldier and picked up the heated bronze. Looking at me intently, he held it in front of my face. Its glow cast an unholy light.

For the first time in my life, I was afraid.

I dislocated my shoulder in a frantic effort that succeeded in pulling me back about an inch. I was quickly repositioned, tightened and in a single, practiced, terrifying and eternal moment, one half of the world went black. Screaming and unable to move, burning bronze took the rest of my vision away from me forever.

I woke on the ground with feet still chained, my shoulder throbbing but bound close to me in a makeshift sling. Reaching up, I felt cloth covering my eyes.

The next few months were a cycle of food, sleep, manual labor in the prison mill and a searching of the soul. I revisited every memory and prayed for God to deliver me to death. At some point, I came to the conclusion I deserved everything I had received and the litany of my failures became my morning and evening prayer.

I am Samson. The one who dishonored my mother and father. The one who broke and disdained the vows of the Nazarenes. The one who touched things unclean. I am Samson, the greedy, Samson the hungry. I am Samson, the violent and ill-tempered judge of Israel. The one who ruled with vengeance and impetuousness instead of wisdom and prayer. I am Samson, whose strength can lift a spoon of cold gruel to my lips and whose life is dependent on the mercy and provision of my enemies. I am Samson the selfish, husband of Philistines and speaker of lies.

I am Samson the weak, Samson the shorn, Samson the forsworn. I am the blind child of the God I ignored and took for granted. My victories are the bones of a tomb. My memories are the faint heat of stone giving no comfort from sweet summer days. I am Samson, the judge who has been judged and found wanting. I am Samson, the miller of grain. I am the one who is hopeless, the one who waits to die.

For weeks, I continued in a place even darker than my blindness could ever know. In the midst of that time, God spoke to me gently.

And my hair began to grow.

My spirit was encouraged by the thought that I was just a man, but God was the God of everything. He knew the generations of my ancestors past. He knows the children of Israel's future. His Hand is not weakened by my failure or thwarted by the plans of His enemies.

In that thought I found hope, and in hope I found His Spirit surrounding me and comforting me again. I found a belief that God was still mine, and I was still His and in darkness my heart was opened.

Not through strength, for I had none. Not through victory, for I was utterly defeated. Not through power or leadership, or judgment. Not through action, or battle or any good I could do. Yet He loved me.

He loved me, just because I was His and not because of what I did or didn't do.

Chapter 16 | Samson Sifted

It wasn't about what I could do. It was about being the man He called me to be and loving Him with my whole heart: as Judge, as son, as husband, as prisoner.

It was never about muscle and sinew. It was never about revenge or power. It was never about my sense of victory of the things I could achieve. It was about God's purpose in the earth and my part to play. In many ways I succeeded; my faith and passion were great. In many ways I failed, selfishly focused on the moment.

Humbled, I became stronger than I ever was in health and victory. Blinded, I saw more clearly than I ever thought possible.

My strength was never my own.

My strength is His.

I am empty, and I am broken. But I have one last prayer to pray. May God use me up completely and let His will on earth be done.

> *"Then Samson called to the LORD and said, "O Lord GOD, please remember me and please strengthen me only this once, O God, that I may be avenged on the Philistines for my two eyes." And Samson grasped the two middle pillars on which the house rested, and he leaned his weight against them, his right hand on the one and his left hand on the other. And Samson said, "Let me die with the Philistines."*
>
> *Then he bowed with all his strength, and the house fell upon the lords and upon all the people who were in it. So the dead whom he killed at his death were more than those whom he had killed during his life"* (Judges 16:28-30).

CHAPTER 17

Saul Sifted

Being king was the best thing that ever happened to me. Along the way, it got harder. But I held on to my position with everything that was in me. Giving up wasn't an option. I was the king! That was all that mattered.

Grabbing a skin of wine, I took a long drink to help me sleep, if you can call it sleep. Perhaps God would speak to me in a dream as He so often had in the past.

I saw the confident outline of a shepherd boy, tanned and strong with the lean and easy movement of someone who spends their days working outdoors. He moved with grace in his worn, hand-me-down clothing. His hands were nervously twisting the leather of the sling at his side.

Our ridiculous champion had come to kill a giant, and I suited him in heavy armor against my men's objections. He couldn't move, he wasn't strong enough to lift it, so carelessly, he left it behind. Then it began. The stones, the shout, the sprint, the throw, the fall, the roar of Israel in victory, the rout of our enemy and the boy again. Raising that terrible sword, the giant sword, he took the head of the one who dared mock the God of heaven. Turning back to me with those blue gray eyes, the sword he could barely hold, covered in blood, he raised the sword again.

Raising it over my head now. Why am I kneeling? How did I get here? His laughter rings as he leans into the cut . . . I screamed and jerked violently . . .

Awake. The sun was shining through the flap in my tent, and I was drenched in sweat. I could see tiny motes of dust coursing in the beam of light, floating, ever floating. Cursing, I sat and tried to shake the nightmares from behind my eyes.

David. How I hated that traitor, trying to take my kingdom away from me. Doesn't he know I am the anointed one? Doesn't he know I am the king? God picked me! A mealy little shepherd boy from a low house won't take this away from me.

I exploded in anger, grabbing a spear and with a maddened cry, I thrust the sharpened end at the lit brazier, spilling hot coals onto the tent floor. I watched them smoke and smolder, giving off a thick, dark, pungent scent. I wondered if the world would burn. I wondered if David would burn with it. As the blaze quieted, I came back to myself. Dressing quickly, I met my men for our counsel of war.

A battle was coming. Our enemies had gathered, and rumor said the traitor David was in their midst. We staged at Gilboa, at the foot of the mountains, as my captains and I went to a high place to look out over the Philistine host. They outnumbered us by thousands and when I realized our situation, my heart crumbled completely. Sudden terror gripped me as the icy hand of death ran his sinuous fingers down my spine. A cold wash of fear flooded over me and with tears in my eyes, I turned quickly to my tent, ignoring the calls of my men.

Lighting a lamp, the illumination seemed too dim, as if the light itself was somehow being swallowed up and couldn't escape. I hunched over to see if I could brighten it, but nothing worked. The very world was growing darker. I watched as the shadows began dancing evilly on the canvas, swallowing the feeble light of my hand. And I prayed, or tried to. I inquired of God if we should go and fight. Would He help us on the morrow?

But God is cruel. He doesn't answer when we need Him most. That made me angry, too. How dare He not answer me! I am the king! Does He not care about our kingdom?

Well, if God wouldn't deliver us, then I would take things into my own hands. My dreams were cold. My prophets were mute. Everyone was watching me, shaking their heads and wringing their hands around me. I needed Samuel. Samuel was dead. I needed him. I needed someone who could bring him to me.

I needed a medium.

So, we found one. She was a practicing witch from Endor, and she could speak to the dead. I needed to hear, I needed to know. I had her call Samuel and when the prophet appeared, she cried out in fear.

This wasn't what she expected.

As the holy prophet of God thundered away at me, I sank to the floor spent and terrified. My worst fears were realized, and the voices of my torment were right. It was too late, and I had gone too far to turn back.

In the morning light, the day of our death found me buckling on the armor of a king. I knew then what I did not know before. God's silence was to check me, to drive me back to Himself. He wanted me to wait, to fast, to pray and to seek Him again. He wanted me to rest in the truth I knew and to obey the Word I had been given. Even as I knew it, I rejected that path forward. I would go my own way. I would pay my own price. If Israel paid it with me, so be it.

It was pride. I was focusing on the power of my role, hanging onto it above all else. I held it above even my own relationship with God and His favor.

> *"And Samuel said, "Why then do you ask me, since the Lord has turned from you and become your enemy? The Lord has done to you as He spoke by me, for the Lord has torn the kingdom out of your hand and given it to your neighbor, David"* (I Samuel 28:16-17).

CHAPTER 18

David Sifted

She was beautiful, and I wanted her. There was nothing else in the world.

She was pregnant, and we had to hide it from her husband. He would never know.

The cover-up didn't work. So I orchestrated an "accident" in battle. No one would ever know. But I knew. And a wife in mourning knew.

And God knew. It's a horrible truth, but He loved me too much to let me get away with it.

I couldn't sleep. I couldn't eat. Everything normal in life was filtered through a lens of guilt and hidden shame. People applauded me taking her in and providing for her when her husband was killed. I smiled and spoke the words they wanted to hear.

They didn't know I had killed him.

People were happy at our wedding; we made such a beautiful couple. We would make such beautiful children. When she started to show, they smiled and praised God for a coming child. They prayed for a prince to make my house even stronger.

They didn't know what I had done.

Stories of Sifted

She was in denial, focusing on caring for the coming child to the exclusion of everything else. It was all too much to deal with on the surface, so we pretended that everything was what it appeared to be. Even to each other when no one else was around, we never spoke of what we had done.

Days turned to months, and the seasons changed. The whole earth moved, but I was stuck. Everything around me came and went as it always had, but sleep still wouldn't come.

It was a boy.

When Nathan came, I thought he wanted to congratulate us on a son. Instead he knew. He knew! And in judgment, he stripped everything away. My child would die, strife and bloodshed would never end for me, and disaster after disaster would haunt my family.

When he became sick, I became broken.

My kingdom, my voice, my songs have all become the ashes of this mourning. I've turned against You and against my friend. I've betrayed the trust of my people and my family. Even her. I can see in her eyes the words unspoken, the sorrow of her grief. It's more than I can bear.

Please be merciful, don't let my son pay the price for my mistakes.

The sky was calm, a stark counterpoint to the silent storm within the palace walls. Outside my door, people were arguing in whispers. I couldn't make out the words, but listening intently I heard the sound that was causing so much fear.

It was the sound of a baby was not crying.

Oh, my Lord and my God . . . I can feel the five smooth stones in the palms of my hands. I can feel the warmth on my face, the shining sun of His presence as I dance into the city.

Yet in the dark of night as I sit alone, the miracle isn't in my grasp. It feels like the miracle will never be in my grasp again. I'm trapped in this waking dream where the giant wins and the ark remains lost with our enemies. I'm trapped in a night where morning never comes. Is this how my story ends?

Is this how all stories end?

I know nothing but this: God's love is bigger than our biggest mistake.

His love is not turned away when we fail. When I feel His presence, He is with me. When I feel nothing but the cold wind of silence, He is there. No despair is beyond His reach.

So I will place my heart in His hands.

> *"Cleanse me with hyssop and I will be clean;*
> *Wash me and I will be whiter than snow.*
> *Let me hear joy and gladness;*
> *Let the bones You have crushed rejoice.*
> *Hide Your face from my sins*
> *And blot out all my iniquity"* (Psalm 51).

CHAPTER 19

Jonah Sifted

God called.

I ran.

The days of my attempt to escape are both a blur and a painting etched in exquisite detail on the canvas of my mind. The storm in its fury, the fear of the sailors, the waves reaching up to meet me . . . all leading to being eaten alive and dragged into the depth of the ocean.

I can't describe the next few days in a way you could understand. Complete darkness filled with barely breathable air. I was surrounded by a sense of directionless motion, interrupted by snatches of exhausted sleep, incredible thirst and at some point, a sense of peace.

There is something freeing about giving up completely. To finally and irrevocably surrender control of the situation was the best thing that's ever happened to me. When God spoke to me, I responded with all of my heart. Everything was stripped away, and it was just He and I.

When I was propelled back into the light, I immediately set my steps to Nineveh. I never would have predicted what would happen next.

Stories of Sifted

It was the greatest revival of my generation. I saw more than 100,000 people set aside their sin and selfishness. I watched as an entire city turned back to God. It's frightening and humbling to see something go so far beyond your true ability. But the spark of revival was a direct result of my speaking. When He turned me back again and gave me a second chance, I found my voice and my stride.

Empowered by the Spirit, I spoke with a supernatural boldness and I could feel His words burning within me. Those days were swept along before a thunderstorm of His justice. Their actions were evil, and I told them so. Their time of accounting had come and destruction, richly deserved, was only a few weeks away. Forty days until God brought holy vengeance and they would pay in full for the evil they had become.

The message didn't bring the result I expected.

Instead of ignoring the word and mocking me . . . instead of hearing it with trembling and despair . . . they responded with greatness of heart. Instead of shirking blame and responsibility, they embraced their own sense of true remorse in the stark face of wrongdoing. Even though it was too late, they repented and they repented with all of their heart.

That's when it happened. God swept through an entire city, and they responded to Him with one voice. It was amazing and I've never seen anything like it, before or since. Repentance and divine compassion combined to restore an entire people back to the Lord.

I've never been angrier at anything in my life.

They were brutal, and they deserved to die. They killed my friends and family and overran the nation that I love. The people chosen to bring blessing to the earth were nothing but a playground of terror to them.

Our women and children were opportunity for use and evil pleasure. Thousands died beneath the sword of their aggression and scorn.

They were not my brothers. They were not my friends. I would rather have died myself than witness them avoid the justice they had earned.

In some sense, that's exactly what happened. I had to die as the person I was to be reborn as the man God was reshaping. His compassion to me in the deep was borne of the same wellspring as His kindness to a city of strangers. My judgment of God's Word over an evil city became a prophesy over my own heart. Like so many things, I didn't see it coming until it was already done.

Do I dare cling to life in a time of disobedience and promise God my heart and hands, while denying that prayer to someone else? Is God the God of the whole earth or just of the people I choose? Is God the God of all people, even the people who don't deserve to be saved?

He gives. And He takes away.

He speaks to cities. And He speaks to me.

He wants my heart even more than He wants my words and grudging outward obedience. He wants me to understand His working even more than He wants me to be comfortable and OK. The days of darkness beneath the water were just the beginning of my truly being able to see.

God's calling is not about my preference. The people I hate are the people He loves.

And His work shapes me even as it shapes the nations.

> *"Those who cling to worthless idols*
> *Forfeit the grace that could be theirs.*
> *But I, with a song of thanksgiving,*
> *Will sacrifice to You.*
> *What I have vowed I will make good.*
> *Salvation comes from the Lord"*
> (A Prayer from the Deep, Jonah 2:8-9).

DOUBT AND FEAR

CHAPTER 20

Noah Sifted

Called to Build

There comes a time in God's calling when you discover that you simply can't accomplish anything on your own. That moment came early for me.

God had clearly spoken to me of a catastrophe to come. The evil of my generation was about to come to a tragic end. Walking with Him, like my fathers before me, was the best thing in my life yet I've never experienced sorrow like I felt in anticipation of the flood. Was it really too late? Was there no other way? Even as I questioned, I knew in my heart this was right. It was like the knowledge of a dream, present without explanation or cause.

The task didn't make any sense, and the enormity of it was almost beyond imagining. I was to build an ark, on dry land, with the blueprints coming from the mind of God. We were to build, we were to gather, we were to trust and the project would take generations.

As I moved to obey, I realized I didn't know where to start. I didn't have the tools or the material. I didn't have the needed expertise. In fact, no one had the expertise. God was doing something new. Waters

Stories of Sifted

would come and cover the earth, and the island of safety for a remnant of creation would fall under His protection.

The mystery was this: Why did God need me to build anything? He spoke the universe into creation, and the heavens moved in their places according to His Word and will. He could speak, and it would be so. Why hand off the most important task in the world to amateurs? At some point, it hit me. It is His pleasure to work in us and through us. His plan is not dependent on our ability. It's only dependent on our ability to trust and obey. That much I could do.

So we gathered materials, we gathered animals and learned what we could on the way. And what a ridiculous way it was. Even in the face of the most solemn task ever attempted, there were moments of laughter and a sense of this being beyond us. How do we find the animals we need to bring? What do they eat? How do we close the door? Where will the water come from? Where will it go? Do we draw straws for who gets to clean up after the giraffes? Anybody have any giant boat building tools we can borrow?

Let me be perfectly clear. Our neighbors were not laughing "with us." Folks for hundreds of miles would stop by to mock at our ship without a shore and the animals beginning to surround us. I couldn't blame them. In fact, I was heartbroken. They hadn't walked with Him. They didn't—they couldn't—understand a world where this made any sense. It hurt to know that the people with their lives and stories and families would never understand, at least not until it was too late. We could only do our best. So we started, even without clearly seeing the whole picture.

For years, we prepared and eventually were ready to start laying the framework. God was faithful and at every step, He guided us directly, making possible the impossible and leading us in the moment to prepare for what came next.

We built, we found every animal we could and tried to learn on the way. Many simply came, and God gave us favor beyond our comprehension. We worked as season gave way to season and year gave way to year. Generations passed, the work continued, with no outward sign that anything would ever be any different. We could feel it though. There was a sense of holy anticipation that the day was coming, and all would be as He said it would.

When the day came, we had everything aboard and God Himself shut the door. I have to tell you that the next few days were terrifying. The wind and the sounds we heard were alien things; even the depth of our trust and the relief we felt at God being true was strained by the enormity of what was happening. When the ark lifted and began to move, we knew what it meant.

Death.

The cities of men and their accomplishments were wiped away in an instant. Nations were scraped clean from the surface of the earth as if they had never been. All was given to the deep. We were buffeted and spun, bounced and swirled on a thousand waves of His judgment and presence. The myriad of life around us was strangely quiet in the days we floated on the ocean of the world. There was a weight to it, a sense of cataclysm with an undercurrent of hope difficult to grasp even for those of us who were there. We grieved the world we knew. We ate and slept and hoped for a day when the world could become new again.

When the light of creation came anew and we rested on the mount of His presence, what could we do but built an altar and worship? There were portents beyond our control and there still are. Walking into the footsteps of His presence and power brought us to a place we could never have imagined. It all boils down to this.

My life is not my own. My calling and the task He has led me to are beyond me. The key isn't ability or effort, or a will set into the things our hands can build. The key is surrender.

> *"When the bow is in the cloud, then I will look upon it, to remember the everlasting covenant between God and every living creature of all flesh that is on the earth . . ."* (Genesis 9:14-15a).

Caught in Sin

We had been at our task so long that it felt good to get back to farming again. Reading the seasons and feeling dry earth upon my hands was simple joy. The grapes were in, and we were finally eating fresh food we had grown ourselves. It felt good.

Our wine had run out some years before, and we were just now building back up to what my family would consider normal. I tasted one of the new wines, and it was heavenly. I took a skin and sat watching the sunset, drinking in peace. When that was done, I got another. I don't know that I consciously intended to get drunk, but I have to be honest . . . I wanted, at least for a little while, to forget.

I wanted to forget what had happened, forget the weight of the world that had literally been on my shoulders for generations. I wanted to forget the cities that were now gone. I wanted, for a little while, to forget the friends of childhood that had been swept away in the storm of His judgment. I wanted to forget the wood and the grain and the animals in their sevens and twos. I wanted to forget the earthy smell of creation as we cared for her. I wanted to forget the rocking days on the crest of the waters, wondering when we would see land again.

Chapter 20 | Noah Sifted

I drank. I let go completely. I should not have.

I don't remember much after that.

I woke up in my bed, and the story slowly came to me.

My son had found me naked and alone, passed out in sin and shame. With nothing but evil intent, he immediately ran to tell whomever he could. I sensed he took delight in it.

My other sons were truer. Shem and Japheth walked in backwards carrying a garment and covered me with the honor and the dignity of men who walk with God. They turned their faces away from me, caught in my sin, so they would not even look upon my shame. They brought me to a place of rest and watched over me until I came back to myself.

I walked with God and still do. My failing doesn't change fundamentally who I am and it certainly doesn't change who He is. Don't misunderstand. I have no excuses to give. I own completely my drunkenness and the fact that my actions brought dishonor to God and my family.

The revelation in my story isn't that we're flawed. We knew that already. It isn't that we can't be righteous on our own; that's a given. We need God to help us on our way, and this will always be true. The consideration here is, how do we respond when we find someone caught in sin?

How do you want to be treated on the day you're uncovered? How do you want the men you know to respond when you're the one undone? What action do you want people to take when you have lost all self-control and moved beyond the laws of God and of man in moments or patterns of weakness?

Should we make failings known to other people as quickly as possible? Do we run to tell our brothers? Is it *loving* to further damage families and people for the sake of flaunting the story? Do we laugh and mock and delight in the fall of great men? Do we arrogantly shake our heads and whisper cautionary tales about how they should've known better? Do we pass judgment on them and write off their work and purpose in the earth?

Do we refuse to gossip about the shame of our brothers and friends, our fathers and sons? Do we walk in backwards, carrying the holy cloth of His restoration and grace and seek to protect them? Do we turn our face and treat their dignity as something precious—not to be touched by human hands? Do we bring them to a place of healing and safety?

At some point in this life, you'll find someone worthy of love in a place where they are caught in their own sin. You'll see them in that horrible place where embarrassment and shame replace everything else. You'll have a choice to make.

Do we recognize they are still children of God?

You can approach them with a heart filled with pride and a desire to add evil to evil.

Or you can find your brother and walk into that place backwards, carrying the cloth of redemption on your shoulders. You will have the chance to find the very heart of God in helping even the best of men come back to His presence with honor.

Choose well.

"But Shem and Japheth took a garment and laid it upon their shoulders and walked backward and covered the nakedness of their father; and their faces were turned away, so that they did not see their father's nakedness" (Genesis 9:23).

CHAPTER 21

Gideon Sifted

I was so afraid.

For years we had been terrorized by the nation of Midian, of Amalek and the sons of the east. They were storming brigands and cruel bullying tyrants even down to the weakest one of them. Nothing we possessed was truly our own; nothing we worked for would last. There was no inheritance and no hope for anything better. We cried out to God without confidence or expectation. And He heard us and answered our prayer in a way that we never expected.

Sweat running down my back, I was working harder than I ever had in my life and my labor was doomed before it began. I was hiding in the winepress, sifting grain without wind or purpose. It was an entirely ridiculous and fruitless exercise. You needed an open area to separate the grain from the chaff in the process of threshing it. Instead, the closed area of the winepress choked me with dust and ill-fitting labor. But we had to remain hidden to keep anything at all. Our children were hungry, and we were doing the best we could. Separating the grain from the debris, unable to breathe I worked for handfuls of food and waited for strong men to come and take it all away.

Stories of Sifted

There, in my frustration and failure, the angel came, speaking words of life and hope in my disbelief.

The Lord is with you, O valiant warrior!

There was a weight to his words, a divine sense of something more, and I struggled to accept it, even though I knew it was somehow the truth. I wasn't valiant. I was hiding. I wasn't a warrior, I was a refugee in my own home, destitute of any battle to fight, much less one to win. I wasn't a leader of men. I was alone. With the angel before me, I had a decision to make.

Could this be the way out? Could this somehow be a path to freedom for all of us?

Coming out of myself, I asked for a sign and the angel answered with fire. And just like that, it was done. We won our freedom that day, before we ever gathered an army and before we ever experienced the series of miracles to come. I built an altar and named it *Jehovah Shalom (the Lord is Peace)*. He had brought us victory and peace with His presence and purpose, before we ever picked up a sword. I knew it deeply, beyond what my eyes could see.

In spite of my spiritual resolution, I still somehow struggled with mental questions of doubt and fear both of which were powerful enough in their own ways. Asking for sign after sign for reassurance, the Lord patiently brought me from where I was to a place where courage became an option. It slowly became something I could dare to reach for, even if it wasn't yet attained. There was no valor in the days of putting out fleeces; they were just my stalling and lack of faith. He had spoken. I had heard and agreed. In my weakness and fear, it wasn't enough. I wanted to hear it again.

And again.

How many times do we ask for one more confirmation before the moment passes and we are truly lost? Will the angel shake his head in sorrow and eventually sit beneath another tree, to speak holy words to someone else, someone who will actually hear them?

I tore down the places of evil worship at night, afraid of my family's retaliation. I was dismayed at the dissolution of our army of men—those who felt exactly like I did. We went from 32,000 to 10,000 to 300 in a rush of backwards momentum I secretly feared meant quick defeat. I began to think we were just a footnote in Israel's story of oppression for another generation.

His Voice was with us every step of the way. But I had so many questions. Undoubtedly, men were afraid; they were outnumbered beyond counting! Why would it matter how people took a drink when they were thirsty? I doubted my own sanity more than once, but we pressed on to see what the next step would bring.

God had promised us victory, but God also knew my heart. I was still afraid.

Thinking back, going into the camp of the enemy was one more useless fleece. Even so, hearing the dream of the man and his sense of dread, it became one more sign that God was with us. With pitchers and torches and the clarion sound of trumpets, a handful of men brought a nation of locusts to its knees. Light, sound and escalating chaos turned the night into a cacophony of bloodshed. But none of it was our own.

He had done it. We were free.

In spite of my reluctant courage and stumbling faith, we had won.

We have the chance for greatness in the evidence of our souls before any battle is set or finished. We are shaped and completed internally before our plans ever become something that others can see.

There is a razor-sharp moment, dividing the infinite distance between hesitation and action, where the mind leaps forward in boldness or the opportunity passes and can never be retrieved. The point of real decision is in the heart *before* the words are spoken, *before* the action is taken . . . *before* the stage is set or the results are known.

Don't be afraid. Your calling begins with the smallest grain of belief that things can be different. They can and they will.

Say yes. Build your altar on the simplicity of the moment before you, and know that God gives good gifts even to the weak.

> *"When the three companies blew the trumpets and broke the pitchers, they held the torches in their left hands and the trumpets in their right hands for blowing, and cried, "A sword for the LORD and for Gideon!"* (Judges 7:20).

CHAPTER 22

Daniel Sifted

We don't see clearly how we fit into the tapestry of our generation. Know that God has a plan and that you are an important part of it, even if you're not entirely sure what it is.

And pay attention to dreams.

I am Belteshazzar, one of the Chief Commissioners, Overseer of 120 satraps and prefects who in turn oversee the administration of Darius. Our kingdom is Babylon and we are the rulers of the known world. Belteshazzar is the name they gave me as a youth, after the sack of Jerusalem. They taught me Chaldean and instructed my friends and me in the service of the royal court. Over the years, I've been promoted to a place of prominence and influence. The riches and extravagance surrounding my daily life are beyond what I ever would have dreamed as a boy, especially a boy who was a slave.

That's on the outside. In my heart, I am a child of Zion, born of the tribe of Judah. The windows of my home open toward Jerusalem and I look to her as I offer prayers to God. I ask for the will of heaven to deliver us. I pray for the Return.

I am Daniel, and I am a prophet of the Most High God.

I was strangely at peace on the day I was to die. Surrounded by God's presence and favor, I didn't lose heart or cry out when the sentence was passed, and they threw me off balance into a den of hungry lions.

I landed, rolled and crouched, expecting the worst. I wouldn't be the first servant of God who died at the hands of the nations, and I knew I wouldn't be the last. Waiting for the attack that never came, I saw him. It was the angel of the Lord standing before me, terrible in his beauty. I was struck by emanating waves of holy power flowing from his very being. I can only say that somehow, he belonged. With his influence over this place of death, I belonged as well. The presence of God was thick like incense and the lions were at rest. It didn't take long before I was at rest as well.

The big cats are surprisingly soft and warm, though it's clear soon enough how very strong they are. Even in repose, and even when they had accepted me, it was still obvious they would never be domestic. I suppose the God of creation formed lions when the earth was young and it shouldn't surprise me that they still remember Him. I watched as the light dimmed when they closed the den, and I listened as the seals were put into place. At that point, there wasn't much to do, so I expressed my thanks to my Father and to His angel and settled in to rest.

In surrender to sleep, as so many times before in my life, I dreamed the dreams of God.

It was a stark contrast to previous days, when the dark night of the soul had been my constant companion. I had slept fitfully when I slept at all and I had been fasting, seeking answers and His direction.

Political enemies were plotting against me, and none of my options were good ones. I considered simply going to Darius directly. The

Chapter 22 | Daniel Sifted

venomous satraps and evil men were trying to pass a law targeting me specifically and trying to entrap me in religious scandal. As I searched for clever counter moves and searched my heart for answers, I felt like God was telling me to be still. It was odd, but my sense was to do nothing in my own defense. My path was to stop trying, stop speaking and to simply allow God Himself to defend me.

Trusting with everything I had within me, it was still a very dark couple of days. With the way things were unfolding, it would likely cost me my position and my life. I started the process of setting my house and affairs in order. My will was set and sealed, and I included a special note for Darius, telling him not to blame himself and to trust in God.

You always hope that if the time comes to lay down your life, that you'll do that with honor and courage. You hope that even the act of dying will bring glory to God and that it won't be in vain.

But how do you know you won't crumble when faced with the choice?

Renounce God or die.

It's easy to claim boldness when things are good and you're comfortable in your own place, resting in familiar surroundings. How do you really know unless you step into that place for real?

When the decision was made, an interesting thing happened. My mind became perfectly clear. My heart stopped racing. I knew that if I died for Him, it would be a part of His purpose and His plan. If He delivered me, that too would be to His glory.

I loved God more than I loved my own life. I loved Him either way.

That note rang like a bell in my heart. It cut through the darkness, and the dread accompanying my season of sifting faded like a barely remembered dream. Who I was simply wasn't based on the outcome of circumstances around me. My relationship with God was all I would ever need.

Like so many things, the dream was His before we saw it in the light of day. The awesome movement of His power ended with the proclamation of a king and the undeniable miracle of His protection.

It had started with loyalty and His work in the heart of a single man.

> *"A stone was brought and placed over the mouth of the den, and the king sealed it with his own signet ring and with the rings of his nobles, so that Daniel's situation might not be changed. Then the king returned to his palace and spent the night without eating and without any entertainment being brought to him. And he could not sleep.*
>
> *At the first light of dawn, the king got up and hurried to the lions' den. When he came near the den, he called to Daniel in an anguished voice, "Daniel, servant of the living God, has your God, whom you serve continually, been able to rescue you from the lions?"* (Daniel 6:17-20).

CHAPTER 23

Esther Sifted

Fear is the greatest roadblock to fulfilling our purpose in life.

It seems that it is always lurking, waiting to paralyze us into inaction or to push us in a direction that ultimately leads to ruin. It is a darkness that feeds on doubt and the insecurity we hide from everyone but our deepest selves. At our core, the will to move, or the surrender to not even try, may be the first and best battle we ever face.

My life was perfect in many ways, surrounded by peace and an environment designed to make my heart as lovely as my appearance. The rolling and angry chaos within was carefully buried and known only to a few.

I was surrounded by the smell of saffron and wild flowers, placed in my chamber by those in charge of caring for my anteroom. It was beautiful. It was quiet. I needed a place to gather my thoughts and even more, to gather my courage. I looked for my heart among the scents and silk clothing, but my hands only found empty adornment.

My cousin had informed me of the plot against our people, an evil scheme borne of our enemy Haman, an advisor to the king. Standing against Haman, we had searched for an opportunity and Mordecai was convinced that our best course of action would come through me. I wasn't so sure.

I had asked him to gather people to fast and seek heaven for three days, while my friends and I did the same. It wasn't just stalling, but I admit that I needed some time. I needed more time than I had available; things were moving too quickly.

The knowledge that I was a Jew was a secret about to be revealed. I took a deep breath and closed my eyes. Maybe I could wait a few minutes more.

I was afraid of failing. Not just for myself, but for the thousands of people counting on me. I was afraid of death. But again, it wasn't just my own life that was a sinking weight upon my heart; it was the death of my people. I hoped for things to reverse, for a people that desperately needed redemption to find it. I was afraid they would never see the answer they longed to embrace.

What if our plans failed? What if the response wasn't what we hoped for? What if nothing happened? What if he was angry and I made things worse? What if I came at the wrong time and sealed our fates forever? We were a city about to be bathed in blood and loss, what could a girl do to stop it?

I could do nothing but try.

I drew myself up to my full height and took a deep breath, releasing it slowly. I raised my hands toward heaven in supplication one last time. Then I stepped forward into the inner court and waited on my king's response.

It is a glorious and frightening moment when you've done all you can and all that is left to do is wait and see what happens. It may only be a few seconds, but that sliver of time contains everything. My wisdom is not as great as my beauty, but the counsel I give is this:

Be afraid. The danger is real. It's not just a shadowy exercise of the mind.

But don't be mastered by your fear. Act as if things will go as you hope and pray that they will. It will give heaven the opportunity to move in you and through you.

Your people need you more than you will ever know.

> *"On the third day Esther put on her royal robes and stood in the inner court of the palace, in front of the king's hall. The king was sitting on his royal throne in the hall, facing the entrance. When he saw Queen Esther standing in the court, he was pleased with her and held out to her the gold scepter that was in his hand"* (Esther 5:1-2).

CHAPTER 24

Nehemiah Sifted

No.

Sometimes you just have to say it.

No!

It's not enough to think it. You actually have to say it out loud. With those first two steps down, you then have to say it where people can hear you.

It's a word that I hated. I've come to know that a well-placed "no" can be ordained by God and is often the key element in accomplishing what He's called you to do. Know "no." It will bless you and your calling.

When my brother told me about Jerusalem, I wept. How could the people God loves be in such disarray? Mourning led to resolve, and through grief and prayer I felt my heart temper into a divine purpose to act.

With the call of heaven and the blessing of my king, I gathered resources and a team of people and went to the city He had put on my heart. I was their leader, and they looked to me for decisions and

Stories of Sifted

guidance. It was a wonderfully terrifying time in my life that I wouldn't trade for anything.

When we surveyed the city, it was like I was looking into the soul of our nation. We were broken, covered in rubble, devastated completely. It was impossible to bear. We had to do something. So I gathered my people and made the call.

Let's rebuild the wall.

The response came from somewhere deep within us. With one voice we agreed and set to organize the project as best we could. Combined with the vision to rebuild, the broken stones before us became the hope that things could change.

Things went well, better than I could have hoped. It was clear God was aiding our effort. Families were each working on their section of the wall, and it was coming together. Those early weeks were filled with hope and sweat.

At some point—there's just no other way to say it—we were tired. In any large project, there comes a point where it seems like it will never end. Clearing the rubble was cumbersome, and the cycle of clearing versus the cycles of building were all but impossible to manage. In addition, we were afraid of being attacked before the wall could be completed. People were losing heart. The work was slowing. They were asking me for help, asking me for a break in the effort.

It was the first time I had to say "no." It was harder than I thought it would be. I was exhausted, too.

Stopping the work to rest and reset wasn't the right way to go. We were at such a delicate and vulnerable time in the process. Stopping would

Chapter 24 | Nehemiah Sifted

have been defeat, but we did need to change our approach. We had to work differently to protect the people involved.

I set guards to protect our families. I had workers carrying tools in one hand and a sword in the other. I constantly encouraged our folks to not lose heart, to not give up, to not be afraid. God was with us. He would help us. He would protect us.

We hit the halfway point, and it turned a corner. Suddenly, there was less work left to do than we had already accomplished, and the possibility of actually completing the wall filled us with renewed determination. At that point, neighboring leaders, threatened by our progress, sent me a request for a meeting.

It was the opportunity for my second "no."

I was tempted though. Maybe I could stall or distract them or reassure them or talk them out of attacking us long enough to get the walls to a position of strength. I wasn't unfamiliar with the political posturing of such attempts, but somehow, I felt strongly that I should stay. Four more times they approached me, threatened me, tried to slander what I was doing.

Four times I gave them a polite and deliberate "no."

My people needed me more. God's work needed me more than my own ego needed to say "yes" and try to talk down our opposition.

In seven weeks and three days, we built a wall three stories high and more than a mile in circumference. It was miraculous. It was clearly not something we could have accomplished on our own. It was the second-best thing God did that year.

Stories of Sifted

For in seven weeks and three days, something even more amazing happened. God called us back to Himself. We read His words to us and renewed the promise and agreement He made with our fathers. It was the most marvelous "yes" of my life.

But the provision, the miracle, the redemption of our generation was set free by a single word. I believe that if I hadn't found the strength to say it, God would have found another way to build the wall.

It wouldn't have been through me. A single word was my strength and the key to releasing God's power in my life:

No.

> *"So the wall was completed on the twenty-fifth of Elul, in 52 days. When all our enemies heard about this, all the surrounding nations were afraid and lost their self-confidence, because they realized that this work had been done with the help of our God"* (Nehemiah 6:15-16).

CHAPTER 25

John the Baptist Sifted

Do you know what the worst thing about prison is? You can't see the sky.

I could handle the injustice and the rough treatment of guards who hated me as part of their assignment. I could handle the whispering of people who knew my legend but had never spoken to me. I could handle the lack of physical comfort, or a good place to rest. But I missed the sky. I missed the open air of the wilderness that was my tabernacle. It was a blessing I didn't expect when God called me away from the city. I loved being away from the noise and the crowds and away from the stench of Roman rule.

In this gray cell there was no escape, and I had a sense that my chapter was about to close. My disciples and friends came often to try to encourage me, but I was in the depth of despair. I was so sure it was Him, sure I had finally found the Messiah . . . for years, I was convinced that Jesus was the One. But recently, my doubts seemed stronger than my resolve.

Outwardly, I tried to put on a good show. I growled and told the guards to repent before it was too late. I don't know if that had any effect, or even if they understood.

Stories of Sifted

Inside, the overwhelming weight of my calling was more than I could bear. From the time I was a child, even before I was born, God's Spirit had been on me for a specific and unalterable purpose: to prepare the way for Messiah to come. My entire life, I was dedicated for ministry, and I was led to a complete commitment to His purpose. My childhood wasn't a childhood. It was an intense time of training for the work to come. Even when His Spirit led me to the wilderness, it was ordained. People came from everywhere seeking to hear the bold words of God that were my heart and teaching.

There were no crowds here. There was no purpose here. There was no water to baptize here. I couldn't escape the thought that I was wrong, that He wasn't the One, that I had missed the path that God needed me to walk. Were my parents wrong or deluded? Was it ego that had led me to believe I was so important to God's work?

I was so sure He was the Messiah when He came to be baptized and the heavens opened. For weeks I felt a foot taller, excited that the time had finally come! Now we would see God in flesh, come in His power, and nothing would ever be the same. The fanfare of God's Kingdom was deafening in my heart.

And then, nothing happened.

In the weeks and months that followed, nothing had really changed. Herod still ruled. The Romans ran their administrations and government as they always had. The Pharisees still abused people from their empty nests of slithering influence and power. This wasn't the Day of the Lord that our fathers prophesied. The weighing and measuring of the world weren't happening in any way I could see. Again, the horrible thought came unbidden to my soul: Jesus might not be the One. Messiah would sift the world and bring righteousness to the whole earth. The coming king had to be more than an itinerant teacher wandering around Galilee, didn't he?

For two days I stopped eating and sleep wouldn't come. Sitting in shadow and weak from my fast, I tried to will myself into God's presence and wisdom. For the first time in a long time, I felt nothing and had no direction. The boldness I was known for lay broken in the dust around me. In the depth of my discouragement I asked God to let me die. Even that prayer went unanswered. I finally found enough strength to act. It was desperate, but I had to have something to hold on to. I needed to know.

But I was trapped here. I couldn't even seek Him out myself.

I had no sky.

I told my disciples to find Jesus and ask Him directly if He was the One or if we should wait for another. Their eyes filled with fear, and they spoke in quick, measured words, trying to reassure me with empty encouragement. I resolutely told them to go. They eventually agreed but were clearly shaken by my bearing and sudden lack of conviction.

As they left, I waited again. I waited for a sign and looked for some semblance of hope. Like prophets and psalmists and great men before me, in distress I asked God my questions . . . and I waited for a real answer.

God isn't threatened by our human nature. He made us and knows us better than we know ourselves. He isn't angry at honest questions, and He wants His will for our lives even more than we do. When you desperately need an answer, ask. When you need direction, seek. Waiting on God, in the scriptural sense, is an active stance of expectation and prayer. So I waited.

Stories of Sifted

I looked toward the beautiful blue of a sky I couldn't see. I reached for the warmth of a heaven I couldn't feel through the cold and rough gray stone of my heart.

I gathered my skins around me and waited for word from a King.

> *"Go back and report to John what you hear and see: The blind receive sight, the lame walk, those who have leprosy are cured, the deaf hear, the dead are raised and the good news is preached to the poor. Blessed is the man who does not fall away on account of me"* (Luke 7:22b-23).

CHAPTER 26

Jesus Sifted

Tempted to do Good

It was clear to me as my Father led me into my ministry and purpose that I wasn't just going to be their Savior. I wasn't just to be their King. I wasn't just their Lord and Messiah, I was something much more intimate.

I was to be their Example.

It was good to see John. He was really coming into his own, and I was proud of the man he had become. God was blessing him, and it did my heart good to see him prosper, even if the world didn't see him with my eyes. When we rose out of the water, heaven itself spoke over me, confirming the calling I knew:

This is my Son, whom I love; with Him I am well pleased.

And peace descended on us like a dove.

It was a peace before the coming storm. From spending time with John, I went to spend time in the lonely desolation of the desert. There I fasted 40 days and 40 nights, bringing myself to the limits of human endurance. Things change after two to three days without food, and hunger subsides—at least hunger in the normal sense. It becomes more dangerous, and every hour you can literally feel the resources of the body being stolen away, bringing a sense of mortality to the fore. I was physically weaker than I had ever been, but it was necessary. This was the stage for my struggle with the Morning Star.

I had spent my days in prayer, study and meditation in preparation for the test to come. Most recently, I had been with Moses, and God's words to Him were life to me. Even reading and still at peace, I began to set my heart for the tempter. It was almost time.

The first trial was to move to satisfy my own hunger through supernatural means. It was a real temptation; I was on the edge. *Just turn these stones into bread*, and in my mind's eye I could see it happening. With that one act, I could move to alter creation for my care. Even more, I could move to feed all hungry people everywhere. I somehow knew that I could just will it to be so, and it would be. No more poor. No child would ever be hungry again. The voice of my enemy whispered to me, and it sounded so right.

But it wasn't what the Father was doing. I responded with the words of the first prophet of Israel:

It is written: "Man does not live by bread alone, but on every word that comes from the mouth of God."

Then my enemy took me to Jerusalem and led me to the top of the temple tempting me to prove myself through miraculous means. By throwing myself down and allowing the angels to save me, preventing the frustration of God's purpose through accident or injury. It was so close to what I was being called to do. It was so close to the signs and wonders of His presence confirming the Kingdom was at hand. It was so close.

Chapter 26 | Jesus Sifted

But it was wrong, and it left the taste of ashes in my mouth. I gave him Deuteronomy again:

It is also written: "Do not put the Lord your God to the test."

Immediately the world blurred, and we were on top of a high mountain. In the distance I could somehow see and perceive the kingdoms of the earth. In this unholy moment, I saw the roads leading to Rome, the cultures of the East, even the cities of people across a great ocean, all being brought together under my rule. I could unite the earth and end injustice. I could bring wisdom and power to law and the organization of government. I could speak out God's very Word and will to the nations of the earth and by bowing to Me, they would be bowing to Him.

All I had to do was compromise.

Turning away from the good I could do, I closed my heart to my rightful place. I could see it too clearly. The earth longed for the direction I could bring. It was the good that Father wasn't doing yet. In perfect symmetry, the words of Moses burned again in my mind, and I spoke them with fiery presence:

Away from me, Satan! For it is written: "Worship the Lord your God, and serve Him only."

Finally, he left me, and I collapsed in exhaustion. Angels came and surrounded me with their strength and power. I thanked God the moment was past.

It wasn't just for me, this test. It was for all who would come after. I prayed they would receive the account of this and make the most of the steps they were called to walk.

Stories of Sifted

The calling and position of God is not for our benefit or comfort.

The ministry of our work is never just a spectacle, bringing a large following through illegitimate means.

The Kingdom of Heaven has no place for compromise with the enemy, even when it seems good.

The Word of God is our strength.

Father, let us do Your will . . . and let Your children follow me in the love and grace You intend.

> *". . . but whoever practices and teaches these commands will be called great in the Kingdom of Heaven"* (Matthew 5:19b).

Crucified for Every One

It was one of those moments that happens, but your mind doesn't accept at first. I felt the sharp pain set in, and I felt the bones of my hand and arm move aside from the metal in excruciating detail.

My back was on fire. I was cold from the loss of blood. I couldn't move or find any position that didn't make things worse. This continued for what seemed an eternity. The other arm was pulled and set. They lifted me up, dropping the crossbar into place with a thud. The cold metal ripping through my feet caused a wave of nausea that passed through my entire body.

When it came to pain, the Romans were skilled.

At some point the level of agony started to lack focus, except for an occasional spike from my hands, or feet or back. Worse, the position of the cross left me unable to breathe. I had to pull on the spikes of my hands and push on the spikes of my feet, raising up to take in a mouthful of air, then collapse back down in a whirlwind of unbearable agony. Every time feels like it will be the last. I could feel the world getting smaller. The end was very near.

The pain was surprising in its intensity and complexity. There was no escaping it, only a futile and continuing effort to try to find any sort of relief. But that wasn't the worst part.

The worst part was the real reason I was here. This wasn't just an ill-timed and unjust execution. The worst part was the cup I was about to drink.

Imagine this.

From the beginning of time, God takes the sin of humankind and places it in a cup without ending or limit. Within the cup, the offenses rest: the rape of the innocent; the theft of a neighbor; the evil thought that passes in a moment; the selfish day spent wasting time; the murder of a wife; the oppression of an entire people; the unwanted infant discarded and left to die.

And still they come: the covering lie; the adulterous secret; the fraud of a stranger; the evil word spoken to wound; the abuse of a child; the girl selling herself for money; the worship of Moloch demanding children for the fire; the random act of destruction; arson destroying a home.

And even again: the foul taste of cowardice; the torture of a prisoner; the delight of a serial killer anticipating the next victim; the petty comment; the husband left for another; the anger that strikes out at a child; the greedy manipulation of harvest; leaving people to starve; the unending litany of the vile; the queue of the actions of the damned; the seemingly unbroken and unending line of evil thought, evil action, evil consequence . . .

All put into the cup of God's awareness and judgment. The cloying taste of that draught would choke all of humanity forever. It was a cup filled with the smell of death and fear and lust, the taste of blood and horror and cruelty, with all the vomit-filled evil the world had ever known. It was a cup prepared for me. Struggling to breathe, struggling to live a bit longer, it was the cup of God's judgment. It was the inescapable truth of His holy power and wrath.

I had to drink it.

I had to drink it all.

I had to bear within myself the darkness and rightful punishment for every ill-intended thought or action. I had to feel His pleasure and presence taken from me as the price was paid. The physical agony was nothing compared to the agony of my soul. Standing proxy for the evil of every man was a desolation of heart, and there was no escape from it. I had to drink it all.

When my task was complete and the moment was finally over, it was blessed relief to feel the favor and love of my God again. The weight of the moment passed and with trembling I surrendered to the extremis of physical limits I had carried this day.

It was finished. I was judged. I was beaten and mocked and punished. I suffered the ignominy of the Romans, even bore the anger of God as a substitution for others. I submitted to humiliation and torture and horror and pain beyond the limits of pain. I drank the cup of His wrath. Death came to close my eyes.

Chapter 26 | Jesus Sifted

I was sifted.

For you.

> *"As the Father has loved me, so have I loved you. Now remain in my love. If you obey my commands, you will remain in my love, just as I have obeyed my Father's commands and remain in His love. I have told you this so that my joy may be in you and that your joy may be complete. My command is this: Love each other as I have loved you.*
>
> *Greater love has no one than this, that He lay down his life for his friends"* (John 15:9-13).

SECTION TWO

FOUNDATIONS IN SIFTING

Defining the Nature and Scope of Sifting

CHAPTER 27

Why Sifted?

*"Simon, Simon, Satan has asked to sift all of you as wheat.
But I have prayed for you, Simon, that your faith may not fail.
And when you have turned back, strengthen your brothers."*
(Luke 22:31)

He was successful in business, and in his new non-profit career he was the natural leader of the group. He was often set apart by the founder, indicating some special anointing. He was the first in the group to confidently call Jesus "the Messiah, the Son of the Living God." He was the only one to step out of the boat and try to walk on water. He was even called out by Jesus as the one upon whom He would build His church.

Peter was full of zeal, pursuing the greatest cause of his lifetime. Although he'd sacrificially left everything behind to follow Jesus, his new life of significance had him riding a high. He said he'd do anything for Jesus, including fight to his death. He was a Type A, High D (on the DISC profile), self-starter and entrepreneur.

He was, in many ways, the profile of most church multipliers. And like most leaders, he was about to experience loneliness, discouragement,

Stories of Sifted

grief, fear and a host of other emotions. He would even question and deny his calling. He would be "sifted!"

At the Last Supper, Peter was part of the group arguing over who was the greatest disciple. Just a few hours later, Jesus rebuked him three successive times for not staying awake to watch and pray as sorrow overcame Him.

During the last supper, Jesus said, "Simon, Simon, Satan has asked to sift all of you as wheat. But I have prayed for you, Simon, that your faith may not fail. And when you have turned back, strengthen your brothers." But Peter replied, "Lord, I am ready to go with you to prison and to death." Jesus answered, "I tell you, Peter, before the rooster crows today, you will deny three times that you know me" (Luke 22:31-32).

Over the next 12 hours, Peter's world was rocked, and he did deny Jesus three times. From pack leader and chosen one to disgrace and confusion in an instant. God used the experience to prepare Peter for what was to come in building His church. God needed a more fully surrendered disciple. He had some character work to finish in Peter. He needed a disciple who would lead from his own position of weakness and God's position of strength rather than in his own power. He needed a man who'd be stronger by being broken.

While Peter had three years to train at the feet of Jesus, the painful process of "sifting" needed to happen to produce the man God intended to use in accomplishing His bigger purposes.

Peter and Judas faced very similar troubles for three years. Both were sifted (the Luke passage tells us Satan asked to sift all the disciples). Peter survived, but Judas did not; Peter turned back and did strengthen his brothers. In some people, sifting leads to strength and Kingdom impact. In others, it leads to weakness and even death. Sifting does not equal seasons of simply surviving trouble. Even pagans do that. It does equal seasons of trouble that produce increased surrender to and trust in Jesus! We are changed in the process. Biblical sifting is intended to accelerate our becoming more like Jesus.

Church multiplication can be hard, lonely and discouraging. It has its share of trouble. The journey is not for the faint of heart. More than 4,000 new churches start each year, which means upwards of 20,000 planters are in the trenches in years one to five. Many of these leaders have considered, are considering, or eventually will consider quitting. Most planters will at some time feel like Peter did the morning after denying Jesus three times.

In a landmark national report issued by Exponential, planters universally cited the following struggles: (1) the internal battle to overcome pride, self-reliance, drivenness and an uncoachable attitude; (2) loneliness and isolation; (3) mistrust; (4) lack of rest; and (5) maintaining joy. That was almost 10 years ago, yet conversations and other studies still indicate that these continue to be major struggles among church leaders.

Should we be surprised that God would use seasons of sifting to grow His church leaders?

Although most church leaders understand the importance of making personal development, soul care and family nurturing top priorities, these things often get lost in a pastor's busyness. The result is a fragile foundation for dealing with the discouragement and loneliness of planting. Eventually, any unresolved family of origin issues or weaknesses in the marriage will surface, often in the midst of a leader's other struggles.

Many simply are not prepared to see these struggles as a season of sifting through which God intends to grow and strengthen leaders. Many become tired and seek to avoid or ignore the sifting rather than embrace and confront it. Unfortunately, too many become hindered in their own strength.

In the next chapter, we'll take a deeper look at the biblical context and a working definition of "sifting."

CHAPTER 28

What is Sifting?

As we've already discussed, sifting is vitally important in Christian leaders' lives. In a nutshell, sifting is unavoidable. It's the weapon of choice God uses to accelerate the spiritual growth of His children. Contrary to our natural human inclinations, embracing sifting, and even pursuing it, is a catalyst for growing more like Jesus.

Still, most of us prefer to avoid it. We'd rather pursue new innovations, new strategies and other tactics to grow our churches. The hard work of personal sifting is simply not sexy. It's messy. But it's unavoidably necessary as a foundation for healthy reproducing leaders.

Jesus promised Peter that it was upon him that He would build His church. The sifting that came through Peter's three denials was a necessary refining of his character to prepare him for the role Jesus promised. In looking at Peter before and after this season of sifting, we see a more humble, but stronger, leader emerge.

Jesus' promise that, "In this world you will have trouble" is universally true. Trouble in this life is unavoidable. But sifting uses trouble as a catalyst to transform our hearts, refine our character and draw us closer to God.

Stories of Sifted

Trouble and trials are not to be avoided, but rather embraced.

Increased surrender pleases God. Sifting yields increased surrender.

> "**Sifted** (v) \ sift-ed 1. Accelerated spiritual growth in times of trouble. 2. Increased trust in God and surrender to His sovereignty. 3. Refined and cultivated seed for increased fruitfulness and multiplication. 4. The seemingly painful process through which every child of God has or will face trials that result in being broken and refined, strengthened and restored, and grown and empowered for God's glory and Kingdom expansion."

Biblical Context

> *"I baptize you with water for repentance. But after me comes one who is more powerful than I, whose sandals I am not worthy to carry. He will baptize you with the Holy Spirit and fire. His winnowing fork is in His hand, and He will clear His threshing floor, gathering His wheat into the barn and burning up the chaff with unquenchable fire."* (Matthew 3:11-12)

> *"Simon, Simon, Satan has asked to sift all of you as wheat. But I have prayed for you, Simon that your faith may not fail. And when you have turned back, strengthen your brothers."* (Luke 22:31-32)

These New Testament passages introduce the agricultural terms "threshing floor," "winnowing fork," "wheat," "chaff," and "sifting." In Jesus' day, the threshing floor was the place where sheaves of grain were crushed under the feet of oxen. The partly threshed grain was continually turned over with a fork. The stalks became broken into short pieces and the husks of grain separated from the stalk. The mixture of chaff and grain was then thrown into the wind with a winnowing fork. The chaff blew away and the good grain collected in a pile. The stalks were often burned.

The entire process is about refining the good wheat from the bad parts of the grain. The refinement that sifting yields makes the grain usable *and* creates seed for producing future harvest—a harvest producing 100 times more crops. Without the sifting, the good wheat is essentially useless.

Both John the Baptist and Jesus refer to sifting as a process of refining good from bad. And as most of us can attest, the process of personal sifting continues beyond our conversion throughout the rest of our lives.

CHAPTER 29

Jesus on Sifting

What did Jesus have to say about sifting?

Some Personal Questions to Set the Stage
(candidly consider your answers):

1. At the end of the coming year when you look back on your accomplishments and what God has done through you, would you prefer to boast of (1) becoming more like Jesus, or (2) doing more for Jesus? If you're like most leaders, you'll say "becoming more like" versus "doing more for."
2. Does Jesus care more about you becoming more like Him *or* doing more for him? The paradox is that the more like Him we become, the more effective we naturally become at doing more for Him. In general, becoming more like Jesus will produce more fruit in the doing more for Jesus. But the reverse is not necessarily true. Doing more for Jesus does not guarantee that we will become more like Him.
3. Consider the books, blogs and articles you've read, the conferences you've attended and the prayers you've prayed in the past year. When you look at the "content" you're drawn to (and the bias of your time), do you tend to focus on resources that help you "become

more like" or resources that help you "do more for" (or do more effectively)? If you're like most leaders, you have a natural affinity to focus on resources that help you do more things, more effectively.

Seasons of sifting have inherent power to shift our natural bias from "doing" to "being." As a result, we tend to see accelerated spiritual growth during these times (think back to our working definition of sifted in the last chapter). It's the secret code the Apostle Paul and others discovered in the first-century church: Trouble is a given. God is our only hope. Pray. Trust. Surrender. Joy. Invite and celebrate more trouble.

It's why the Apostle James says, "Consider it pure joy, my brothers and sisters, whenever you face trials of many kinds, because you know that the testing of your faith produces perseverance. Let perseverance finish its work so that you may be mature and complete, not lacking anything" (James 1:2-4).

"Pure joy!" Seriously? For many of us, sifting is a painful thing to be avoided. Pure joy? Hmmm. Maybe we need to take our sifting more seriously and embrace it more wholeheartedly.

Learning from Jesus

Through His life examples and His words to the disciples, Jesus gave us some truths about being sifted—promises that we can continue to count on when we're facing trials and temptations.

Jesus promised trouble.

In John 16:33 Jesus says, "In this world you will have trouble." He doesn't say "maybe" or "If you're lucky, you will avoid it." In His final documented series of prayers for believers, Jesus didn't even ask God to spare us of troubles. Instead, He asked God to protect us from the evil one when the times of trouble come." Ephesians 6 is all about putting on the armor of God; verse 13 specifically says, "so that *when* the day of evil comes" we would be prepared. It doesn't say "*if* the day of evil comes," but rather "when." We should expect and anticipate trouble.

Jesus experienced trouble Himself.

Jesus doesn't expect us to go through more than He did. He faced troubles of all kinds. In Matthew 26:36-38 we read, "Jesus went with His disciples to a place called Gethsemane, and He said to them, 'Sit here while I go over there and pray.' He took Peter and the two sons of Zebedee along with Him, and He began to be sorrowful and troubled. Then He said to them, 'My soul is overwhelmed with sorrow to the point of death. Stay here and keep watch with me.'"

In John 13:21 Jesus is troubled by losing one of His disciples: "After He had said this, Jesus was troubled in spirit and testified, 'Very truly I tell you, one of you is going to betray me.'"

There is rest in Jesus during our momentary troubles.

In John 14:1 Jesus says, "Do not let your hearts be troubled." In John 14:27 He says, "Do not let your hearts be troubled, and do not be afraid." In Matthew 11:28, He encourages us with, "Come to me, all you who are weary and burdened, and I will give you rest."

Embrace trouble; avoid worry. They are different.

Jesus is blunt about worry and its value. In Matthew 6:25-34 (parts) He says, "Therefore I tell you, do not worry about your life, what you will eat or drink; or about your body, what you will wear. Can any one of you by worrying add a single hour to your life? But seek first His kingdom and His righteousness, and all these things will be given to you as well. Therefore do not worry about tomorrow, for tomorrow will worry about itself. Each day has enough trouble of its own."

Taking up our cross to follow Jesus is an overt act of trouble.

In Matthew 16:24 Jesus says, "Whomever wants to be my disciple must deny themselves and take up their cross and follow me." The context of His call to action was not one of lush, stress-free living. He called the disciples to a life of worldly trouble for advancing the Word.

In Matthew 13 Jesus tells the parable of the sower. In describing the man (seed) who is not firmly rooted he says, "When trouble or persecution comes because of the Word, they quickly fall away." Note two key points: (1) "*When* trouble or persecution comes" —again, it's not a question of "if" but "when," and (2) "because of the Word." Jesus tied our trouble to the work of advancing the Gospel. He expected His followers to have trouble because of Him and His message.

"The battlefield of sifting is in the mind!"

Our primary challenge is the enemy's battle for the captivity of our mind (not the trouble itself).

Consider Ephesians 6:12: "Our struggle is not against flesh and blood, but against the rulers, against the authorities, against the powers of this dark world and against the spiritual forces of evil in the heavenly realms."

Troubles are of the flesh and blood; worry is the overflow of the trouble rattling around in our heads. Satan seeks to take our minds captive to fear, worry and anxiety amidst our troubles. In John 16 Jesus told the disciples they would have trouble in this world. Hours later when praying to God for the disciples He said, "I have given them your Word and the world has hated them, for they are not of the world any more than I am of the world. My prayer is not that you take them out of the world but that you protect them from the evil one" (John 17:14-15).

Jesus could have asked God to keep trouble away from the disciples (take them out of the world). Instead, He asked God to protect them from the evil one when the trouble came. Jesus was keenly aware that our battle in sifting is of the mind.

CHAPTER 30

Paul on Sifting

The Apostle Paul knew trouble. From flogging to hunger to imprisonment to fear of death, he faced it all and through it all said, "In all our troubles my joy knows no bounds." In, through and because of his sifting, Paul learned the secret to "being content in any and every situation." Let's look at 10 truths about sifting that we learn from Paul's life and words.

10 Learnings on Sifting From the Apostle Paul

1. *You can run, but you can't hide.*

    "I am convinced that neither death nor life, neither angels nor demons, neither the present nor the future, nor any powers, neither height nor depth, nor anything else in all creation, will be able to separate us from the love of God that is in Christ Jesus our Lord" (Romans 8:38).

    We may run from God during our troubles, but we cannot run from His love. It is unconditional regardless of our troubles or our response to them. Sifting sometimes makes us angry with God or leaves us questioning Him. However, sifting can never separate us from His love. He waits with open arms.

Stories of Sifted

2. *God comforts us in our troubles.*

   "Praise be to the God and Father of our Lord Jesus Christ, the Father of compassion and the God of all comfort, who comforts us in all our troubles, so that we can comfort those in any trouble with the comfort we ourselves receive from God" (2 Corinthians 1:3-4).

   While God allows us to experience troubles, He provides comfort. He is not selective. Paul notes that he comforts us in "all our troubles."

3. *Sifting reinforces our dependence on God.*

   "We were under great pressure, far beyond our ability to endure, so that we despaired of life itself. Indeed, we felt we had received the sentence of death. But this happened that we might not rely on ourselves but on God, who raises the dead. He has delivered us from such a deadly peril, and He will deliver us again" (2 Corinthians 1:9-10).

   Paul clearly states that the purpose of trouble he experienced was to increase his reliance on God. Often our sifting is intended to break our strong nature or tendency to control things in our own power. A core tenant of sifting is God's desire for us to rely fully on Him. It's in our most helpless circumstances that we most aggressively reach out to Him. He desires our passionate pursuit in all circumstances.

4. *An eternal perspective guides us through sifting.*

   "We are hard pressed on every side, but not crushed; perplexed, but not in despair; persecuted, but not abandoned; struck down, but not destroyed. We do not lose heart. Though outwardly we are wasting away, yet inwardly we are being renewed day by day. For our light and momentary troubles are achieving for us an eternal glory that far outweighs them all. So we fix our eyes not on what is seen, but on what is unseen, since what is seen is temporary, but what is unseen is eternal" (2 Corinthians 4, parts).

Paul encourages us to focus not on what is seen (the physical world, the trouble, the temporary situation), but rather on the eternal. His eternal perspective allowed him to see terrible trouble as "light and momentary."

5. *Advancing the Gospel guarantees trouble.*

    "As servants of God, we commend ourselves in every way: in great endurance, in troubles, hardships and distresses, beatings, imprisonments and riots; in hard work, sleepless nights and hunger; through glory and dishonor; in bad report and good report, genuine, yet regarded as impostors, known, yet regarded as unknown; dying, and yet we live on; beaten, and yet not killed; sorrowful, yet always rejoicing; poor, yet making many rich; having nothing, and yet possessing everything" (2 Corinthians 6, parts).

    Imagine this list as a job description. Paul blatantly says that the cost of being a servant of God is trouble. There is simply no getting around it.

6. *We can experience joy in the trouble.*

    "I am greatly encouraged; in all our troubles my joy knows no bounds" (2 Corinthians 7:4).

    Even in the best of times, it's difficult to comprehend joy that knows no bounds. To experience this level of joy amid terrible troubles is a testament to the power of the Holy Spirit within us. The same power that raised Jesus from the dead is alive and at work within us during our seasons of sifting. If we allow it, that power produces joy.

Stories of Sifted

7. *God's power is made perfect in our weakness.*

    "In order to keep me from becoming conceited, I was given a thorn in my flesh, a messenger of Satan, to torment me. Three times, I pleaded with the Lord to take it away from me. But He said to me, "My grace is sufficient for you, for my power is made perfect in weakness.' Therefore I will boast all the more gladly about my weaknesses, so that Christ's power may rest on me. That is why, for Christ's sake, I delight in weaknesses, in insults, in hardships, in persecutions, in difficulties. For when I am weak, then I am strong" (2 Corinthians 12:7-10).

    In times of sifting, we are vulnerable. Our weakness spotlights God's power, bringing glory to Him. Through our weakness, we can shine the power and perfection of God during our troubles.

8. *Contentment is possible in all circumstances.*

    When sifted, we seek to get beyond the season as quickly as possible. We can become discontent amid trouble. Paul shows us a better way:

    "I have learned to be content whatever the circumstances. I know what it is to be in need, and I know what it is to have plenty. I have learned the secret of being content in any and every situation, whether well fed or hungry, whether living in plenty or in want. I can do all this through Him who gives me strength" (Philippians 4:11-13).

    As believers we also know the secret.

9. *Trouble is certain; timeline is uncertain.*

   "And now, compelled by the Spirit, I am going to Jerusalem, not knowing what will happen to me there. I only know that in every city the Holy Spirit warns me that prison and hardships are facing me" (Acts 20:22-23).

   While Paul was certain that trouble would continually face him, he did not always know what form it would take or when it would occur.

10. *Sifting requires us to focus and persevere.*

    "Therefore, since we are surrounded by such a great cloud of witnesses, let us throw off everything that hinders and the sin that so easily entangles. And let us run with perseverance the race marked out for us, fixing our eyes on Jesus, the pioneer and perfecter of faith" (Hebrews 12:1-2).

    Church leaders experience a multitude of external troubles that hinder ministry (e.g., finances, facilities, leadership, etc.). Additionally, we carry internal character issues (sin) that weigh us down. Paul encourages us to "throw off" these external and internal issues and focus on Jesus. During our seasons of sifting, we will likely need to deal with these issues while fixing our eyes on Jesus. And yes, Paul acknowledges that we will need perseverance to finish the race.

CHAPTER 31

Causes & Symptoms

Asking Why: Discerning Causes from Symptoms

Think about the last time you went to the doctor for a physical and all the measurements they did: height, weight, pulse, temperature, blood pressure. A few days later, you probably received a report indicating "normal" standards and where your results stack up. For those of you who haven't had a physical in a while, think about your car's dashboard and all the measurements: temperature, oil, tire pressure, battery charge, speed, RPMs, mileage. Measurements give us insights into the health of our bodies or condition of our cars. When those numbers or amounts are abnormal, we set out to understand why.

It's important to distinguish between symptoms and causes. A 101°F temperature coupled with aches and pains are symptoms a doctor uses to diagnose underlying causes. Often, we take temporary remedies (e.g. pain reliever, cough medicine, heating pads, etc.) to alleviate symptoms and help us tolerate them until the root causes work their way out our systems.

Sometimes in life, the troubles we face (the symptoms) naturally take care of themselves without us needing to address root causes. However, in many cases we continually struggle until we get to the real issues.

Scripture repeatedly reminds us that God often chooses the symptoms (troubles) to get our attention to address the underlying causes.

Consider the Apostle Paul and his affliction: "In order to keep me from becoming conceited, I was given a thorn in my flesh, a messenger of Satan, to torment me. Three times I pleaded with the Lord to take it away from me. But He said to me, 'My grace is sufficient for you, for my power is made perfect in weakness'" (2 Corinthians 12:7-9).

Paul's symptom (visible trouble) was the thorn in the flesh. Like many of us, Paul was driven in a way that sometimes makes it easy to get ahead of God and trust in our own power. Just as a small "thorn" can cripple us, God allowed Paul to experience physical trouble as a continual reminder of his human weakness.

Our challenge is to continue asking "why" until we get to that root cause. In seasons of sifting, it's particularly important that we slow down, reflect and consider whether or not we are dealing with root causes. What if our prayers changed from, "Please take away the trouble (symptoms)" to "Please reveal to me the root causes of my trouble?"

Underlying causes typically cut right to the heart of our character. In most cases, dealing with them results in heart transformation and increased surrender to God. It's not uncommon for them to be rooted in either personal character issues and/or unresolved family of origin issues.

As we look at our own stories and journeys of sifting, we need to distinguish between troubles (symptoms) and underlying causes. The symptoms are often visible and a great place to start (just as a doctor begins with our easily checked vitals). Dealing with the deeper rooted issues will inevitably take more diligence and hard work that may be at the root of God allowing your season of sifting.

Starting with Symptoms

(Following are some of the more common symptoms)

Below are some of the more common symptoms of sifting that pastoral leaders face. Of course, everyone has a unique story; your story may not fit into one of these categories. The list is simply a tool for filtering your own experience. In which of these areas have you experienced "trouble?" What's missing from the list?

Discouragement
Financial hardship and struggle (draining savings, retirement, etc.)
Loss of key friends/friendships
Inability to gain momentum and growth (hitting barriers and walls)
Failing/quitting (death of the dream)
Isolation (lack of peer fellowship, friends, team, etc.)

Mental Health Issues
Depression/bipolar disorder
Anxiety
Sleeping problems
Abuse recovery

Family Tragedy and Challenge
Death of a child/spouse
Infertility
Rebellious/wandering kids
Disease/serious illness of family members

Marriage
Infidelity and marital unfaithfulness
Marriage tension

Verbal abuse
Neglect
Lack of respect
Conflicting schedules/lack of quality time
Conflicting personal values (e.g., money management, boundaries, raising children, discipline, priorities, etc.)

Personal Character
Pride/arrogance
Humility
Narcissism
Teachability
Idols
Coveting/comparison
Unresolved family of origin issues
Control issues

Workaholism
Burnout
Boundaries
Adrenal Disease or disorder
Accountability (lack of)

Addictions
Pornography
Prescription drugs
Illegal drugs
Alcohol
Technology/Internet

Like the "thorn" in Paul's flesh, troubles are simply the means to God working on our hearts to yield increased surrender to Him. In most cases, the bridge from "trouble" to "surrender" passes through "root causes." Consider reflecting on the "troubles" that may seem to hinder your life and ministry. Do they represent a season of sifting? Are there more fundamental root causes that need to be identified and addressed?

CHAPTER 32

Spiritual Warfare

Did you ever wonder why Jesus, at the age of 27 or so, didn't just sit down and write the New Testament? Wouldn't that have been cleaner for everyone involved? Just skip the manuscripts, translations, canon, councils, re-translations of the NIV, the hoopla and basically be done with it!

Did you ever wonder why God allows us to be sifted at all? Why not protect, or warn or be more active in keeping people from harm?

Have you ever questioned the nature and timing of spiritual warfare? Why does God allow it to hit at the worst possible time? It's rarely when we are rested and ready that the conspiring of adversity comes, with a spiritual weight that simply crushes the soul. Life has plenty of trouble, without any spiritual component in play. The consequences of our mistakes and wrong thinking bring extremely difficult seasons of sifting.

Add to that a real enemy in the spiritual realm, who is smarter, more experienced and who knows our history and triggers better than we know ourselves. The deck is stacked against us. With Satan as a real entity gunning for us, and the battle of the mind we experience, there is no way we can emerge intact without God.

Could it be that the realization of our weakness and dependence is ultimately healthy?

We know God is powerful. The work He did on the Cross is sublime. His resurrection is a story of power and death bowing to holy justice and love. So, if God is who He clearly is, how can there be a real war, with real casualties and real loss? On the spiritual front, there is no lack of ammunition from heaven. And yet the battles are real, the war is real. The intersection of spiritual warfare in sifting is a critical component.

Sifting plus spiritual warfare is a catalyst of opportunity for us to go deep with Him in three primary ways:

First, He wants us to be a willing and active part of the process.

His work in us and through us is not an afterthought, a silent partner scenario or an unearned trust fund account, but an active, vibrant, vital, and integral part of His working. He led Paul, Mark, Luke and others to put real pen to real paper and (perhaps) to really struggle with how to tell the Story best with real words we could understand. He leads us through our character issues and allows us to suffer, to fail and to try again. He leads us to success, to heartache and to a depth of love and courage we never would have considered possible when we began.

He leads us to be a part of the fight, to share in the cost, to step into His passion and His pain and the glory of the gospel of His peace. It's not just a series of blank checks we cash repeatedly with no trouble in sight. We struggle. He leads us to struggle. He allows us to play (or fail to play) a vital part in even the most important work possible—the sharing of His Gospel with our generation.

Chapter 32 | Spiritual Warfare

When we experience resistance, it's too easy to forget that's actually a good sign. Or that the discouraging blow of spiritual warfare can indicate health.

Paul writes in Ephesians:

> *Finally, be strong in the Lord and in His mighty power. Put on the full armor of God, so that you can take your stand against the devil's schemes. For our struggle is not against flesh and blood, but against the rulers, against the authorities, against the powers of this dark world and against the spiritual forces of evil in the heavenly realms. Therefore put on the full armor of God, so that when the day of evil comes, you may be able to stand your ground, and after you have done everything, to stand* (Ephesians 6:10-13, NIV).

It is a mystery that through His grace and in His grace, it is still our part to struggle. The very nature of grace is that we aren't good enough, and we aren't strong enough to win this fight on our own. But even with God's loving, powerful and unflinching assistance, we have some sense that our victory from day to day is not a given. It is His pleasure that the cost we endure be real, that the fight be a real one. As we examine the armor and weapons of our spiritual war, we come to see that the real battleground is in the realm of the spirit, the soul and the mind.

Second, the realization that spiritual warfare is occurring leads us to perceive seasons of sifting differently.

The question we need to ask in a time of suffering or attack isn't, "How quickly can I get out of here?" It's "What does God want me to learn here?" The discipline to not leave the sifting season until we fully absorb its lesson can result in blessing.

Remember that Job's answer came through God's speaking. Job's heart was at rest— before any restoration to his body, his family or any other circumstance. Remember that Paul's answer to his thorn in the flesh wasn't a miraculous delivery but instead a direct word from the Father to endure. Also, think about Joseph and Job processing their sifting years later. Through understanding God's perspective, Joseph turned the evil and tragic circumstances of his life into a positive that his years as a slave and in prison didn't change. And God redeemed Job's memory of his difficult times through His work in Job's heart, as he saw his purpose in the bigger picture.

Don't forget that the thing we carry with us forever isn't the suffering of the moment, but rather the *response* to it. That moment comes and goes, passing from the now into the past beyond our reach. We carry the mark on our soul, good or bad, to our next step, next day and next chapter.

This is why forgiveness is so crucial. There is no better way to keep our past wounds alive than to hold on to them beyond all reason. Years later, the ones who hurt us probably aren't hurting us now. If we continue to revisit that hurt, the pain we feel continues in our heart, transcending the passing of time. Schemes come to frustrate us, orchestrated to trigger past wounding so that we respond disproportionately and without the love of God.

God allows this, not to pour salt into the wound, but to give us an opportunity to look deeper. To, in the light of His love and His grace, lay our hearts bear before Him and allow our character and thinking to be shaped differently. It is a battle in the spiritual realm, and it will often be won or lost as our human heart struggles with itself. Our response to spiritual warfare is an opportunity to be shaped in His image. It's a chance for us to change for the better in permanent ways.

On the surface, it looks like people are out to get us, or circumstances are conspiring to steal our joy. The reality is that God is moving, and our enemy is resisting. Our battle is to look past the flesh-and-blood nature of the problems we encounter and fill our minds and hearts with a response that puts God's armor, weapons and heart in primary position.

Third, we cannot win the fight in the spirit realm on our own. That realization immediately changes our perspective for the better.

Hasn't that been the case in your experience? When you realize, "Hey, wait a minute! There is something deeper going on here. This is a spiritual attack!" Isn't that a turning point? We need help—spiritual help. We need to pray and ask God, surrendering to Him, His love, His hope and His method. That moment changes everything, and it's as much about letting go of our own ability and understanding as it is being active in the right way.

One of the greatest things we can do to win in spiritual warfare is to lock into God's perspective and trust Him greatly. That surrender can set our minds free from worry and let us rest in His peace and presence even when the actual outward circumstance may not have changed. Don't misunderstand. God is powerful. He can move in any way He wants to move. Scripture leads us to ask and to look for God to actually change things and deliver us in real and practical ways. But the battle of the mind will often be won in our hearts—before it is ever realized in the world we see.

The real key to victory is to see with His Eyes. In the day of trouble, we have to look beyond the surface to a layer deeper than we normally consider. We need to respond with a depth that goes beyond the moment and to a place where faith, truth and the sword of His word rule the day.

Prayer plays a vital role in this process. Any prayer is a conscious and explicit acknowledgment that we can't do this on our own. It's no accident that our deepest times of prayer and burden are during times of sifting and warfare. God knows us! He knows that trouble makes us extremely attentive. It isn't trouble for trouble's sake. The good thing we gain by passing through spiritual warfare is worth the cost.

During seasons of sifting and spiritual warfare, we need to be a willing participant in God's will. Let your perception shift to see beyond circumstance into the spiritual nature and timing of the conflict and trouble. Actively surrender to God, acknowledging that the battle in the mind is won through relying on our Father and His path forward.

If we do that, we stand. If we do that, we win. And it is God's pleasure to let us be sifted along the way. Not with cruel intent, or careless neglect, but with a plan of His Gospel and grace borne in us before the beginning of time. Don't give up. Don't be discouraged. Trust Him with everything you have and with everything He has given. Be the person you were created to become.

Stand.

CHAPTER 33

Multiplication

Why are we sifted?

That question (and variations of it) has been asked for 2,000 years: Why does God allow His people to suffer? To what end are we sifted? Why are enduring trials important to us in this temporary life—and to God's overall desire and plan to reconcile us to Him?

When we start to look for these answers, it helps to go back to the agricultural origin of sifting and get a clear picture of its role in the harvest season. In biblical times, the overall sifting process was vital, as it separated the grain from the inedible chaff (the protective casing surrounding the seed). After the fields had been harvested, the cut stalks of grain were brought to the threshing floor where they were beaten or crushed under oxen to separate the grain from the stalks. From there, the broken stalks were tossed in the air, as the wind blew the lighter chaff to one side. The refined, heavier grain fell to one area where it could be gathered—the "fruit" of the harvest. This seed would be replanted and used to produce and multiply future harvests a hundred hold. Ultimately, the sifting process was the first step leading to exponential growth for the years to come.

Stories of Sifted

In the same way, we are sifted and refined through trials and struggles. Like the refined seed separated from the chaff, we also have the potential to bear fruit and multiply. We are called to draw deeply from our own experiences of suffering and use those learnings to encourage others. The outcome of our sifting—the answer to our "why" questions—is intended to be fruitfulness and multiplication.

Think about Peter and that key passage in Luke 21. Fruitfulness and multiplication are inherently built into this scripture. After telling Peter that Satan has asked to sift him and the other 11 disciples, Jesus says: ". . . and when you return, encourage your brothers" (Luke 21:32). It is the picture of a soldier who comes through a battlefield stronger and wiser, ready to encourage and train his comrades to face the same obstacles. One person can initiate a ripple effect. Jesus allows Peter to be sifted, knowing that his testimony will encourage the other disciples when they are sifted—ultimately laying the foundation for the church.

Time and again throughout Scripture, we see this truth. From God's command to Adam and Eve to "be fruitful and multiply," to His promise to Abraham to multiply his descendants, to the Great Commission of Matthew 28, fruitfulness and multiplication are His end intent and promised blessing to those who endure.

How do we experience multiplication?

So, if we understand the intended outcome of sifting, the next question to ask is, "How does sifting produce multiplication?"

How do we walk through seasons of sifting whereby the end result is increased fruitfulness and multiplication? Sifting itself doesn't produce multiplication. Rather, it's our *response* to suffering—our increased surrender and faithfulness—that's key to the equation. As we surrender

Chapter 33 | Multiplication

ourselves and grow in our faith, our head knowledge evolves into true heart transformation. Only then do we bear fruit and multiply.

In Matthew 19, Jesus affirms the impact of our willingness to surrender our will. The rich young ruler has just left and the disciples (led by Peter) have essentially asked what's in it for them. Jesus is clear in His response: "Everyone who has left houses or brothers or sisters or father or wife or children or fields for my sake will receive a hundred times as much and will inherit eternal life" (Matthew 19:29).

A few chapters later, He shares the Parable of the Talents, a clear illustration of the truth that our impact is directly proportionate to our surrender and faithfulness: "For whoever has will be given more, and they will have an abundance" (Matthew 25:29).

And of course, nowhere is this process more clearly portrayed than in the life and ministry of Peter. Through surrender, the disciple experiences true heart transformation that as we know, ultimately became the cornerstone of the church. It is a before/after story like no other. Prior to his denial of Jesus, Peter was a typical Type A, confrontational leader, always quick to pick a fight. When Jesus tells Peter that he will deny Him three times, Peter refutes back, "Even if I have to die with you, I will never disown You" (Matthew 26:35). As the rooster crows, Jesus' earlier words and gaze are not lost on the disciple:

"The Lord turned and looked straight at Peter. Then Peter remembered the word the Lord had spoken to him: 'Before the rooster crows today, you will disown me three times.' And he went outside and wept bitterly" (Matthew 26:75).

In denying Jesus and in the weeks that followed, Peter is broken. When the risen Jesus appears to the disciples and reinstates Peter, we see a surrendered man. Three times, Jesus asks Peter, "Do you love me?" each

Stories of Sifted

time reaffirming His love for the disciple and His faith in him as "the rock" on which He will build His church (Matthew 16:18).

From then on throughout the New Testament, we see a different Peter. Pre-sifted, he had the head knowledge. Post-sifted, we see heart transformation in a man surrendered to God's will. Pre-sifted, Peter lacked the character God wanted in the leader who would build His church. Post-sifted, the experience enabled God to refine character issues. He needed a more fully surrendered leader, a man who would be stronger by being broken. To be prepared for the multiplication ahead, Peter would need to undergo a heart transformation. He would need to be sifted.

As history tells us, Peter's transformation set in motion a global movement of multiplication and influence. Some 2,000 years later, the church started and led by the man Jesus called "the rock" on which He would build His church is incomparable in its exponential growth. Throughout history, the church has been and continues to be the greatest multiplying force to date.

Where does sifting fit into the multiplication process?

So if heart transformation yields multiplication, what part does sifting play?

Think of it this way. Our seasons of sifting provide the context for surrender and heart transformation. The troubles and trials God allows into our lives naturally create magnified opportunity for increased surrender and faithfulness. Again, it's not suffering, but our response to it (surrender and faithfulness), that produces heart transformation.

Consider this. Jesus could have come to earth, called the 12 disciples, proclaimed He was the Son of God, performed a few miracles to reinforce that claim, gone to Jerusalem, predicted His death and resurrection and then fulfilled it—all in one week. He's God. He could have done whatever He wanted. The disciples would have witnessed what they needed to think He was God.

Why did Jesus choose to spend three years with the 12?

He knew that it would take time for what the disciples saw and heard— the head knowledge—to become heart transformation. He knew that for these men to carry out His mission of making disciples to the ends of the earth, it would take three years of the disciples walking with Him, intersecting with worldly troubles and learning what it means to surrender. With only a week, there would have been no sifting, no context for surrender.

The three years were integral to the necessary changes God needed to make in Peter and the disciples. It's a truth we must remember: The work of surrender and heart transformation requires the essential element of time. It is the means by which sifting works itself out. We can't rush the sifting process.

Think about it. With no real relationship to Jesus, would Peter's denial of knowing Him have meant anything or made any impact? Would he have ever been broken? His sifting served as a catalyst to utter surrender of his life and ultimately a heart transformation that would birth the church and multiply its impact and influence exponentially.

> *". . . more and more men and women believed in the Lord and were added to their number. As a result, people brought the sick into the streets and laid them on beds and mats so that at least Peter's shadow might fall on some of them as he passed by. Crowds gathered also from the towns around Jerusalem, bringing their sick and those tormented by impure spirits, and all of them were healed"* (Acts 5:14-16).

CHAPTER 34

Your Story of Sifted

Imagine the course of human history as a great tapestry in the hall of a castle. It is epic in scope, filled with heroes, lovers, children and prophets all making their mark on the world. You see nations and churches, markets and organizations wending their way to greatness and from greatness to decline on the canvas before you.

You start to notice patterns, and a grander story begins to emerge. It is beautiful. The chaos of the individual life starts to make sense when seen in the larger context. Even the suffering and loss are a vital part of the whole. You silently rejoice at the freedom of the human heart, filling its place perfectly and leading to something amazing. You wonder why you never saw it this way before.

You start to follow some of the threads, tracing Charlemagne and the horn of Roland to their place. You see the academia of the Greeks and the practicality of the Romans. You witness the rise and fall of empires: Babylon, Persia, China, the Mayans, the Incas and finally Rome and the rise of the West. You see art and human endeavor, from Mozart to da Vinci to Dante to Shakespeare and more. They add such a lovely counterpoint to the melody before you.

You see cities - wonderful collaborations of civilization as they rise and slowly set. You witness ideas being born and running their course as they shape the ebb and flow of human activity. You notice spiritual men and marvel at the visual thunderclap of Abraham, Isaac and Jacob, sending ripples through the course of human events. You encounter our fathers searching for a city not made with human hands, finding it time and time again. In the center, you see Him and the lines leading to and through Him . . . connecting everything in such a way that brings it all together.

It is overwhelming. It is humbling.

And then something else starts to happen. You see your family and generation after generation leading to the city of your birth. You notice the events surrounding your childhood in a new way, and your context is not accidental. It is perfectly designed and crafted to be a part of the whole. You see the Hand that guides us leading you to somewhere very good. Even the times when you suffered - the dark nights of the soul - become part of the path that ends up being heaven itself.

And you notice the threads around you, the family and friends, the co-workers and the people you love to spend time with. Their stories come to life and they too, contribute to the whole. We see all too dimly the depth of our experiences and shared experiences. Our journey is intended to end well.

Perhaps the most fascinating thing about this book is that it is still being written. All around us, new chapters are springing up as everyone is added to the tapestry of God's purpose in the earth. Each of us has a chapter where we find life and meaning in seemingly dark and terror-filled places. Those moments of realization strengthen our sense of faith and shape the course of our lives.

The great hope with this project is that you've found a poignant resonance with the idea of *Sifted* and that your own suffering or heartache is also being redeemed. We hope that as you've read these chapters and stories, you've recognized aspects of your own story, and that becomes one more reason for joy. With those hopes in mind, we would like to invite you to actively participate in the *Stories of Sifted*.

Your story is not just your own. It intersects with the lives of hundreds and, by extension, to thousands of people around you. As such, the wisdom and encouragement you've found will be a blessing and an aid to the people you meet. The Author and Finisher of faith is writing the book of you, with some chapters completed, some in process and some yet to be written.

The Challenge:

Now what? As you've encountered these stories, we hope you now see seasons of sifting as opportunities for growth and increased surrender rather than something to be avoided. If so, that's great!

Some readers yearn for more than new thinking. You've read the stories of these Bible leaders and through their eyes have discovered elements of yourself and your story. You intuitively know that your stories of sifting are both different and yet mysteriously the same as theirs. In a new and real way, you sense what Paul referred to as "surrounded by such a great cloud of witnesses." The stories of sifting of those heroes of the faith—messed up and sinful people like us—now encourage and strengthen you. It's the fulfillment of Jesus' command to Peter, "and when you turn back, encourage your brothers."

See the cycle? Those who have come before us (and those with us now) experience sifting. They grow through the process and now encourage others, including you. Now you experience sifting. You grow through it and in turn, encourage others. We are all part of this mysterious and godly cycle.

The vital link in this cycle? We must discover and embrace our own story of sifting, and then grow through it to be a blessing and encouragement to others. God wants to use your stories to weaken you to Him so you can be strengthened to those around us.

Listen to what God is saying to you. Perhaps you need to commit to investing the time now to discover and refine your own stories of sifting, surrendering them to God and ultimately using them to encourage and strengthen others.

In the coming weeks and months, we want to challenge you to do three things.

1. Reflect on your own seasons of sifting.

- Spend the next few weeks or months thinking about this process.
- Consider the landscape of your life. How have you been sifted in the past?
- Can you describe these times? Take notes and outline your story.
- Think of your seasons of sifting as a mosaic. How do they fit together? What common themes and elements do you see?
- Are you currently in a season of sifting? Is one about to begin?

2. Write your story (or stories) of sifted.

- Use this opportunity to take what you've been thinking about and put it on paper or screen. You'll start to remember important details, discover turning points, and see it take shape as a whole.
- Rewrite it. Go through it again to sharpen the focus, add transitions and make your experience as clean and as understandable as possible.

3. Share your story with someone.

- Talk to someone you love and trust and process your story with them.
- Use their counsel and feedback to clarify and make your story even more poignant.
- Consider how your story could be used as counsel or encouragement to someone else. . . . Be ready to share your experience!
- Begin to share your story, praying that God will use it to encourage and challenge others. Discovering, refining and telling your story is one of the most powerful things you can do to make a positive impact on the lives you touch.

Remember that most of the Bible leaders you've read about in this book did not for a minute comprehend their place in history. They may have had no idea we would know their names and the events of their lives. In the same way, we can't comprehend the scope of our reach. The love, blessing and stories we share ripple through our network of relationships, impacting others generations deep.

Your story is important. It uniquely and powerfully reflects beauty. Let your seasons of sifting shape and focus that story. Let them refine you and mold your heart and character. Step into a sense of increased surrender until the chapters of your life shine with the gospel of His peace.

Become the person you were created to be—even as you are sifted—and when you return, encourage others with your story!

EPILOGUE

There I was, sailing happily through life when, without warning, along came a ferocious storm. A season of sifting that would in a moment, forever change our family and me.

My son Ross—our only child—was a person of great promise. He was my heir, my successor, and, in ways that may seem odd to you but absolutely real to me, one of my greatest heroes.

On the evening of January 3, 1987, I received a call, "Ross is missing in the Rio Grande." Ross was 24 years old, and it was the last adventure of his life on earth.

I remember walking along a limestone bluff perhaps 200 feet above the muddy and treacherous river, as frightened as I've ever felt. *Here's something you can't dream your way out of,* I told myself. *Here's something you can't think your way out of, buy your way out of, or work your way out of.* It was all too clear in this maddening solitude on the river bluff. *This is,* I thought to myself, *something you can only trust your way out of.*

The incomprehensible was breaking out all around me, and there was no way I could understand it apart from an eternal perspective. Albert Einstein once said, "What is incomprehensible is beyond the realm of science. It is in the realm of God." This was truly in the realm of God.

As horrifying and as sad as it was, and is, to have lost him, Ross' disappearance and death also provided the greatest moments of rare insight and grandest gestures of immeasurable grace and joy that I ever hope to experience. Utter emptiness and brokenness left me feeling awful and wonderful at the same time.

In those dark weeks after Ross' death, I was forced to lean on God entirely, to think often of the Scripture verse: "Trust in the Lord with all your heart and lean not to your own understanding" (Proverbs 3:5). I learned that God truly is sufficient and that His strength is made perfect in weakness. I learned that in my life on earth, I live as:

- A pilgrim not in control
- A steward, not an owner
- A soldier, not with security

While seasons of sifting are unique and personal, we are all united in the common experience of emptiness and brokenness amidst our sifting. It's always easier to see the fruit of our struggles once we've moved beyond sifting's valley of darkness. But in the valley, we often feel lost and hopeless.

My dark days taught me it's essential that we rely on God's compass, His navigation, His hand of protection and His deliverance to bring us through our seasons of sifting. He simply wants us to take our hands off the wheel and give Him control, even when our nature is to grab the controls and hold on even tighter in the middle of the storm and chaos around us.

In those months following Ross' death, I went through a wide range of emotions. Those were very difficult times. It was hard to see beyond the horizon of the deep valley I was living in. But God was faithful, as He always is.

Epilogue

In the eye of the storm, all I could do was trust. In hindsight, I realize that trust produced a new level of surrender that's hard to quantify or define with a formula. I couldn't see it then, but my increased surrender ultimately yielded a more refined seed God could use to produce an even greater harvest.

A profound and unexpected element of Ross' eternal legacy is the increased multiplication made possible in me, here on earth—a noticeable result of how this tragedy transformed my heart and yielded my dreams to God. Our stories of sifting, and their intersection with the relationships weaved throughout them, create ripples of impact for generations, and ultimately into eternity.

In his letter to the Romans, Saint Paul wrote a comforting message, summing up this profound mystery: "We know that God causes all things to work together for good to those who love God, to those who are called according to His purpose" (Romans 8:28 NASB).

I believe without a doubt that all things really do work together for good, but not without an eternal perspective. I can say from experience that your personal stories of sifting—like the heroes of our faith who have come before us—will make profound impact beyond your wildest imagination or dreams. But we have to intentionally embrace those stories and see them through an eternal lens. We must trust.

Bob Buford
Founder, Halftime and Leadership Network
(adapted and expanded from the book *Halftime*)

On April 18, 2018, Bob reunited with his son. His eternal perspective here on earth in the wake of his son's death has been beautifully fulfilled.

ABOUT THE AUTHORS

Todd Wilson
President and CEO of Exponential

Todd is a Kingdom entrepreneur. He spends the majority of his time starting and working with organizations committed to Kingdom impact and multiplication. Todd is a founding member of Exponential, which organizes and hosts the annual Exponential conference in Orlando and live events throughout the United States and world. Todd serves as President and CEO of Exponential, providing vision and strategic direction to the organization. Todd lives in Manassas, Virginia, with his wife, Anna. They have two sons and two beautiful daughters-in-law: Ben (married to Therese) and Chris (married to Mariah).

Eric Reiss
Executive Pastor for The Surge Community Church

Eric serves as Executive Pastor for The Surge Community Church. He is a teacher, author, songwriter, and recording artist with a quirky sense of humor. He's in love with his wife, Karen, and with their well-above-average daughter, Evangeline. He and his family live in Burke, Virginia.

Made in the USA
Middletown, DE
10 August 2019